Scottish
Cakes and Baking

Scottish Cakes and Baking

in colour

Dione Pattullo

Johnston & Bacon

London

A JOHNSTON & BACON book published by
Cassell Ltd.,
35 Red Lion Square, London WC1R 4SG
and at Sydney, Auckland, Toronto, Johannesburg
an affiliate of
Macmillan Publishing Co., Inc.
New York

First Published 1980

ISBN 0 7179 4273 2

Printed in Great Britain by Camelot Press, Southampton.

Contents

Acknowledgements

*Colour photographs by A. L. Hunter
Photography, Edinburgh
Drawings by Jim Proudfoot*

The author would also like to thank the following for their assistance:

The Kitchen Range, William Street, Edinburgh, for the loan of accessories used in the photographs.

Romaine Rae and Mrs Burns for their assistance in the preparation of food for photography.

Mrs Marion Brown of St Fillans, Perthshire, and Mrs Jenny Carter of Edinburgh, for the loan of accessories.

Jenners Ltd. of Edinburgh for the loan of the china used on the cover photograph.

Introduction

Scotland's reputation as a land of excellent bakers is world-wide and, I believe, well deserved; but to a certain extent Scotland has rested upon this reputation, and has been in danger of losing her long-held advantage. Fortunately, all is not lost, for while the multiple bakeries may continue to produce bread which tastes like wet flannel, dry scones and leatherlike pancakes, there has in recent years been a proliferation of small bakers who produce marvellous baps and butteries, and it is still possible to get delicious Selkirk Bannocks and excellent oatcakes; although a really good commercial shortbread is hard to find.

What may be lacking on the commercial side, though, is more than made up for by the excellence of home baking; and in this respect, Scotland's bakery is still a triumph. Very many cooks all over Scotland take enormous pride in the production of delicious tea-time treats, and the exchange of recipes and competitions among friends and local groups constantly contributes to the resources of baking, and keeps alive our heritage. A willingness to experiment and diversify is, after all, essential in all walks of life, and no less in cookery than in any other.

The task of compiling a book on Scottish baking has been something of a challenge. Too often 'Scottish baking' conjures up images only of the traditional dishes—the oatcakes, scones and ubiquitous shortbread. You would really think we never baked anything else. But

new products, new ideas and methods, new shortcuts are coming along all the time, and there is no reason at all why you should not make use of these shortcuts if they do not detract from the quality of the end product. So in this book I have tried to find recipes which are easy to make, quick to prepare—in short—foolproof.

Many people think they can't bake, often because they have tried to do things which were beyond their capabilities at the time. If you are unsure of your skills, start with some of the simple biscuits which are less likely to fail, and then move on to the easy cakes and scones, and you will be pleasantly surprised at just how much you can do. This book is designed to give good basic recipes for home baking for coffee and tea parties, for children's teas, and for enjoyment pure and simple.

While I have been writing, testing and talking about this book, I have been fortunate to have been lent some most interesting and very old cookery books from the kitchens of large Scottish houses. These have been a tremendous source of inspiration, and have been fascinating reading. Many of the recipes have proved to be excellent, and very economical to make. I have adapted a number of them to suit the modern kitchen. Many of the recipes would have fed a small army—and quite probably did—but in smaller proportions they have also worked out well.

Over the years I have also collected many recipes which have become family standbys. These have come from all over the world, and include a number of more glamorous recipes which really deserve the much misused name of 'gateaux'. These may be used very successfully for dinner parties or buffets where a large cake that is easily sliced and served is a boon to the busy hostess. Do not, on the other hand, be misled by the apparent plainess of some of the recipes; I am thinking in particular of the Turkish nut cake, which has no looks, but is truly a delicious experience.

Every recipe in this book has been tried and tested by me. Grammes and ounces have both been given and I have also used extensively the new metric spoon measure. I have in some recipes used cup measures; this is a very simple method of getting the proportions correct, and needs no scales. The cup I have used is the standard 6 fluid ounce cup, but cup measures are available in sets from $\frac{1}{4}$ cup to 1 cup from most ironmongers and kitchen shops.

Lastly, I am well aware that time is of the essence, and no-one has any. But it is amazing how little time it takes to produce a batch of warm scones or pancakes, and how much your effort will be appreciated —so do try. Cakes may take a little longer, but are well worth the effort. So have a go, and I hope you enjoy making these recipes as much as I have enjoyed writing them and testing them.

Quantities

Most recipes in this book are designed to feed 4–6 persons. This depends on the appetite of those fed, or the pocket of the cook.

Approximate oven temperatures

Follow guidance given in individual recipes.

Cool	225°F	110°C	Gas $\frac{1}{4}$
Slow	300°F	150°C	Gas 2
Moderately Slow	325°F	160°C	Gas 3
Moderate	350°F	180°C	Gas 4
Moderately Hot	375°F	190°C	Gas 4
Hot	400°F	200°C	Gas 6
Very Hot	425°F	220°C	Gas 7

Clockwise, from top: Coffee Meringue Cake, Chocolate Cream Roll and Tipsy Orange Cake

Clockwise, from top right: Treacle Pancakes, Potato Scones, Scotch Crumpets, Girdle Scones

From left to right: Scotch Scones, Country Date Scones,
Wholemeal Scones

Scones
& Tea Breads

Any book on baking by a Scot that does not have a chapter on scones must be suspect, so here to ward off suspicion are scone recipes I have found and enjoyed over the years.

Basic rules for scones are as follows. Get your ingredient measurements right, and when rubbing in the fat, be it butter or margarine, use only the finger tips, preferably with cool hands (though I believe that this rule is over-emphasised by many). Almost all recipes may be made with self raising flour, instead of plain flour and the usual bicarbonate of soda and cream of tartar mix. But do not substitute self-raising flour in recipes that include treacle or syrup. Whatever liquid you use to bind the mixture may be partly replaced by an egg, which will make the scones richer and much nicer; this, of course, is not necessary, but it can be a useful way to use the odd left-over egg yolk! Do not worry about the mixture being soft. If too much liquid is added in error, extra flour can quickly be kneaded in. It is useful, too, to remember that scone dough should be soft to produce light scones. A firm dough will produce hard and rather tough scones. Kneading should be light and brief; and finally the oven should be hot.

For those recipes requiring a girdle, heat the girdle over a high heat and turn down to use. A little flour sprinkled on to test its readiness should brown quite quickly.

Plain Scones

200 g (8 oz) plain flour
2.5 ml (½ teaspoon) bicarbonate of soda
2.5 ml (½ teaspoon) cream of tartar
pinch of salt
50 g (1½ oz) butter
150 ml (6 fl oz) milk

Sift together all the dry ingredients and rub in the butter. Use a broad bladed knife to mix in the milk to form a light dough. Knead on a floured board and roll out to ½ inch thick and cut into approximately twelve 2 inch scones. Bake on a floured baking sheet in a hot oven (425°F, Gas 7, 220°C) for 10 minutes.

Royal Tea Scones

500 g (1 lb) flour
10 ml (2 teaspoons) baking powder
pinch of salt
50 g (2 oz) butter
grated rind of 1 lemon
50 g (2 oz) caster sugar
100 g (4 oz) currants
approximately 220 ml (½ pint) milk

Mix flour, baking powder and salt in a bowl and rub in the butter. Add the finely grated rind, sugar and currants. Stir in sufficient milk to form a soft dough. Knead lightly. Turn on to a floured board and cut in bars approximately 2 inches by 1 inch. Bake in a hot oven (400°F, Gas 6, 200°C) for 10 minutes. Take out of the oven, brush with milk and scatter a little caster sugar on top. Return to the oven for a few more minutes until browned. Serve hot. This quantity makes about 10 scones.

Boiled Milk Scones

5 ml (1 teaspoon) sugar
pinch of salt
200 g (8 oz) self-raising flour
25 g (1 oz) butter
150 ml (6 fl oz) milk

Add sugar and salt to flour and rub in the butter. Heat the milk and when tepid pour into the flour. Mix with a broad bladed knife. Turn on to a floured board and knead lightly. Roll out to just over $\frac{1}{4}$ inch thick. Bake on a hot girdle for 4 minutes on each side.

Country Date Scones

200 g (8 oz) plain flour
2.5 ml ($\frac{1}{2}$ teaspoon) bicarbonate of soda
5 ml (1 teaspoon) cream of tartar
25 g (1 oz) butter
50 g (2 oz) chopped dates
10 ml (2 teaspoons) syrup
110 ml (4 fl oz) milk
1 egg

Sift dry ingredients into bowl and rub in the butter. Chop dates finely and add to dry ingredients. Warm syrup with some of

the milk and add to the dry ingredients with egg. Add rest of milk as needed to make a soft dough. Turn on to a floured board, and roll out to $\frac{1}{2}$ inch thick. Using a 2 inch cutter cut out approximately 9 scones. Bake on a floured baking sheet in a moderately hot oven (375°F, Gas 5, 190°C) for 20 minutes. Cool on a wire tray. *Illustrated in colour opposite page 9.*

Wholemeal Scones

150 g (6 oz) wholemeal flour
50 g (2 oz) plain flour
10 ml (2 teaspoons) baking powder
2.5 ml ($\frac{1}{2}$ teaspoon) salt
75 g (3 oz) butter
1 egg
150 ml (5 fl oz) milk approximately

Mix all dry ingredients in large bowl. Rub in the fat. Whisk egg with milk. Make a well in the middle of dry ingredients and stir in milk and egg mixture. Add more milk if necessary to form a soft dough. Turn on to a floured board. Roll out to approximately $\frac{1}{2}$ inch thick. Using a plain $1\frac{1}{2}$ inch cutter, cut out about 12 scones. Place on a floured baking sheet. Bake in a hot oven (400°F, Gas 6, 200°C) for 15 minutes. Cool on a wire tray. *Illustrated in colour opposite page 9.*

Ginger Scones

200 g (8 oz) self raising flour
5 ml (1 teaspoon) ground ginger
2 ml ($\frac{1}{4}$ teaspoon) bicarbonate of soda
2.5 ml ($\frac{1}{2}$ teaspoon) cream of tartar

11

10 ml (2 teaspoons) caster sugar
30 g (1½ oz) lard
1 egg
5 ml (1 teaspoon) syrup
75 ml (3 fl oz) milk

Sift the dry ingredients well together and rub in the lard. Mix the egg and syrup with the milk and add to the rubbed in mix. Form a soft scone dough and roll out into 2 six inch rounds. Mark each round into six with a knife. Flour a baking sheet and put the scones onto it. Bake for 10 minutes at 425°F, Gas 7, 220°C. Cool on a wire tray and eat very fresh.

Nairn Tea Scones

200 g (8 oz) plain flour
5 ml (1 teaspoon) baking powder
pinch of salt
15 g (½ oz) caster sugar
1 egg
milk to mix

Sift flour, baking powder and salt into bowl. In another bowl beat the sugar and egg thoroughly. Sift an extra spoonful of flour on to a board. Now add the beaten egg and sugar mixture to the flour. Add a little milk if needed to form a soft dough. Flour a dessertspoon and spoon out a piece of the dough mixture. Toss the dough into a ball shape in the flour. Repeat. Place on a greased tin, flatten slightly and cook in a hot oven (400°F, Gas 6, 200°C) for 8 minutes.

Treacle Scones

200 g (8 oz) plain flour
2.5 ml (½ teaspoon) bicarbonate of soda
2.5 ml (½ teaspoon) cream of tartar
2.5 ml (½ tablespoon) sugar
2.5 ml (½ teaspoon) cinnamon
2.5 ml (½ teaspoon) mixed spice
pinch of salt
50 g (2 oz) margarine
30 ml (2 tablespoons) black treacle
milk to mix

Mix dry ingredients in a bowl and rub in the margarine. Mix the treacle with a little milk and add to the dry ingredients. Add the rest of the milk as needed to form a soft dough. Knead lightly on a floured board. Roll out to ½ inch thick and cut into rounds. Brush the tops with a little milk and bake in a hot oven (400°F, Gas 6, 200°C) for 15 minutes. Makes about 12 and they keep very well.

Potato Scones

200 g (8 oz) mashed potato
50 g (2 oz) plain flour
15 g (½ oz) butter
pinch of salt

Put potato through a ricer to eliminate any lumps. If a ricer is not available use a wire sieve. Add butter and salt and beat well. Work in the flour with your hands. Dust a board heavily with flour and roll dough out thinly. Use a tea plate as a guide to cut out into large rounds. Cut each round into quarters. Heat a girdle and butter lightly. Put scones on the girdle for 5 minutes on each side. Eat at once with butter. *Illustrated in colour between pages 8 and 9.*

Scotch Scones

200 g (8 oz) plain flour
pinch salt
2 ml (¼ teaspoon) bicarbonate of soda
5 ml (½ teaspoon) cream of tartar
25 g (1 oz) butter
buttermilk to mix

Sift dry ingredients into a bowl and rub in the butter. Add sufficient buttermilk to form a soft dough. Turn on to a floured board and cut into scones using a 1½ inch cutter. Bake on a floured baking sheet in a hot oven (400°F, Gas 6, 200°C) for 12–15 minutes. Cool on a wire tray. *Illustrated in colour opposite page 9.*

Cheese Scones

200 g (8 oz) plain flour
2.5 ml (½ teaspoon) bircarbonate of soda
5 ml (1 teaspoon) cream of tartar
salt
mustard
25 g (1 oz) lard
50 g (2 oz) grated cheese
1 egg
milk to mix

Sift dry ingredients into a bowl. Rub in the lard and then stir in the cheese. Mix egg

and milk and mix into the dry ingredients to form a soft dough. Roll out to ½ inch thick and using a 1½ inch cutter cut out approximately 12 scones. Place on a floured baking sheet and cook at 425°F, Gas 7, 220°C for 12 minutes. Cool on a wire tray.

Whipped Cream Scones

300 ml (½ pint) double cream
200 g (8 oz) flour
15 ml (3 teaspoons) baking powder
3 ml (¼ teaspoon) salt

Whip the cream stiffly. With a fork mix in the sifted dry ingredients and turn on to a lightly floured board. Knead for 1 minute. Roll out to about a third of an inch thick and cut into diamonds with a fluted cutter or plain diamonds with a sharp knife. Bake on a floured baking sheet at 425°F, Gas 7, 220°C for 10 to 12 minutes, until they are a pale golden colour.

Lunch Scones

25 g (1 oz) butter
200 g (8 oz) self-raising flour
25 g (1 oz) sugar
100 ml (4 fl oz) milk, sufficient to mix
1 egg, beaten

Rub the butter into the flour. Add the sugar and bind with the milk and egg mixture reserving a little. Knead lightly on a floured board. Roll out to ½ inch thick. Cut with a 1½ inch fluted cutter. Brush tops with reserved milk and egg mixture and bake on a floured baking sheet (400°F, Gas 6, 200°C) for 10–12 minutes.

Farmhouse Scones

25 g (1 oz) caster sugar
1 egg
60 ml (2 fl oz) vegetable oil
pinch of salt
350 ml (12–14 fl oz) milk
500 g (1 lb) self-raising flour

Mix sugar, egg, oil and salt and whisk lightly. Stir in the milk. Sift flour twice before adding the liquid. Mix lightly. Drop in spoonfuls onto a floured board. Roll into a round shape and cook on both sides on a moderately hot greased girdle.

Wheaten Scones (1)

100 g (4 oz) wheat flour
100 g (4 oz) plain flour
2.5 ml (½ teaspoon) salt
2.5 ml (½ teaspoon) cream of tartar
2.5 ml (½ teaspoon) bicarbonate of soda
milk to mix

Sift all the dry ingredients together and make sure they are well mixed. Form a scone dough with milk. Turn on to a

floured board and cut out into 2 inch rounds. Cook on a hot greased girdle for approximately 5 minutes on each side.

Wheaten Scones (2)

100 g (4 oz) plain flour
300 g (12 oz) wheatmeal flour
40 g (1½ oz) caster sugar
5 ml (1 teaspoon) cream of tartar
5 ml (1 teaspoon) bicarbonate of soda
5 ml (1 teaspoon) salt
25 g (1 oz) butter
milk to mix

Mix the dry ingredients thoroughly and rub in the butter. Add the milk and mix with a broad bladed knife to form a fairly soft dough. Turn on to a board covered with wholemeal flour and knead lightly. Roll out to ½ inch thick. Cut with a 2 inch cutter and bake on a floured baking sheet in a hot oven (400°F, Gas 6, 200°C) for 15 minutes. Cool on a wire tray. Makes approximately 12.

Crulla

25 g (1 oz) butter
½ kilo (1 lb) or more flour
200 g (8 oz) sugar
10 ml (2 teaspoons) baking powder
2 eggs
1 cup milk
few drops vanilla
lard for frying
icing sugar

14

Rub the fat into the flour and add the sugar and baking powder, the beaten eggs, milk and vanilla. This should form a slightly tacky dough. Using well-floured hands take off pieces and form into twists about 2 inches long and not too thick. Fry in deep hot lard. When they rise to the surface, turn them over and brown the other side. Drain on absorbent paper and sprinkle with icing sugar before serving hot.

Drop Scones

Drop Scones

200 g (8 oz) plain flour
5 ml (1 teaspoon) cream of tartar
10 ml (2 teaspoons) bicarbonate of soda
pinch of salt
50 g (2 oz) caster sugar
15 ml (1 tablespoon) syrup
1 egg
milk to mix

Sift dry ingredients into a bowl. Mix the syrup, egg and milk together and pour into the flour. Beat well with a rotary beater to form a pouring batter. Drop onto a hot greased girdle to form some rounds. When bubbles rise, turn over and cook on the other side until brown. Keep warm in a clean tea towel on a wire tray.

15

Girdle Scones

200 g (8 oz) plain flour
2.5 ml (½ teaspoon) bicarbonate of soda
2.5 ml (½ teaspoon) cream of tartar
pinch of salt
50 g (2 oz) margarine
milk to mix

Sift dry ingredients into a bowl and rub in the margarine. Mix to a soft dough with milk. Turn on to a floured board and knead lightly. Roll out and cut into 2 inch rounds. Place on a hot greased girdle and cook until brown, then turn and brown the other side. Allow approximately 10 minutes on the girdle altogether. Cool on a wire tray. *Illustrated in colour between pages 8 and 9.*

Treacle Pancakes

400 g (1 lb) flour
60 g (3 tablespoons) caster sugar
2.5 ml (½ teaspoon) ground ginger
7.5 ml (1½ teaspoons) cream of tartar
5 ml (1 teaspoon) bicarbonate of soda
pinch of salt
25 g (1 oz) butter
15 ml (1 teaspoon) black treacle
milk as required
3 eggs

Sift dry ingredients and rub in the butter. Warm treacle with a little of the milk and beat into the eggs. Pour into the centre of the flour and beat in adding enough milk to form a drop scone consistency. Heat a girdle and grease lightly. Drop by spoon-

fuls onto the hot girdle. When bubbles start to rise, turn pancakes over and cook until done. Cool on a wire tray between the folds of a clean tea towel. *Illustrated in colour between pages 8 and 9.*

Poor House Perkins

90 ml (6 tablespoons) flour
30 ml (2 tablespoons) oatmeal
15 ml (1 tablespoon) sugar
5 ml (1 teaspoon) bicarbonate of soda
15 ml (1 tablespoon) black treacle
milk to mix

Mix dry ingredients. Warm treacle with a little milk and add to the dry ingredients with sufficient extra milk to form a dropping consistency. Heat a greased girdle and drop spoonfuls of the mixture onto it and cook until done–approximately 10 minutes in all. Eat hot with butter.

Scotch Crumpets

1 egg
26 g (1 oz) sugar
150 ml (5 fl oz) milk
100 g (4 oz) plain flour
pinch of salt
5 ml (1 light teaspoon) cream of tartar
2.5 ml (1 teaspoon) bicarbonate of soda
30 ml (2 tablespoons) milk

Beat egg with sugar until thick using a rotary beater. Add 150 ml (5 fl oz) milk,

16

flour and salt and stir in. Dissolve cream of tartar and bicarbonate of soda in rest of the milk and stir in quickly. Pour on to a hot greased girdle in large spoonfuls. Cook until brown and turn over to complete cooking. Keep in a warm clean cloth on a wire tray before using. *Illustrated in colour between pages 8 and 9.*

Doughnuts (1)

50 g (2 oz) butter
150 g (6 oz) plain flour
50 g (2 oz) sugar
10 ml (2 teaspoons) baking powder
pinch of salt
grated rind of 1 lemon
1 egg
milk to mix
additional sugar for final stage

Rub butter into the sifted flour and add rest of dry ingredients. Beat egg with a little milk and mix into the flour mixture to form a light dough. Using two cutters, one smaller than the other, cut into rings. Cook in boiling deep fat until brown on both sides. Toss in caster sugar on grease-proof paper and cool on a wire tray.

Doughnuts (2)

150 g (6 oz) flour
25 g (1 oz) cornflour
5 ml (1 teaspoon) baking powder
pinch of salt
pinch of nutmeg
50 g (2 oz) caster sugar

15 ml (1 tablespoon) corn oil
1 egg
60 ml (4 tablespoons) milk
corn oil for frying

Sift all the dry ingredients into a bowl. Mix the oil, egg and milk in a small bowl and whisk together. Heat corn oil for frying in a deep fat pan. Mix the liquid into the flour mix and form a stiff dough. Knead lightly on a floured board and roll out to a quarter of an inch thick. Cut into $2\frac{1}{2}$ inch rounds and cut a small circle out of the middle. When the oil is heated to 360°F drop them carefully in and turning all the time, fry until golden brown all over. Drain on a paper towel and toss in caster sugar.

Baps

500 g (1 lb) flour
2.5 ml ($\frac{1}{2}$ teaspoon) salt
50 g (2 oz) lard
25 g (1 oz) yeast
5 ml (1 teaspoon) sugar
300 ml (10 fl oz) milk and water mixed

Sift flour and salt into bowl and rub in the lard. In a smaller bowl cream the yeast and sugar. Heat the milk and water to just tepid. Strain on to yeast. Add this mixture to the flour and form into a soft dough. Cover and leave to rise for 1 hour. Knead lightly and divide into rolls. Prove for a further 15 minutes in a warm place. Press in the middle of each bap and brush with milk. Dust with flour and bake in a hot oven (425°F, Gas 7, 220°C) for 15–20 minutes.

17

Spicy Rolls

(to serve with fruit compôte)

400 g (1 lb) plain flour
10 ml (2 teaspoons) baking powder
50 g (2 oz) butter
50 g (2 oz) caster sugar
5 ml (1 teaspoon) ground ginger
25 g (1 oz) carraway seed
275 ml (½ pint) milk

Sift flour and baking powder. Rub in the fat and then add sugar, ginger and carraway seed. Mix to a light dough with the milk. Form into 12 roll shapes with floury hands. Place on a floured baking sheet and cook at 375°F, Gas 5, 190°C for 12–15 minutes.

Brown Loaf

150 g (6 oz) plain flour
150 g (6 oz) wholemeal flour
10 ml (2 teaspoons) cream of tartar
5 ml (1 teaspoon) bicarbonate of soda
25 g (1 oz) margarine
25 g (1 oz) syrup

Grease a 2 lb loaf tin thoroughly. Mix dry ingredients well and rub in margarine. Add syrup with enough milk to make a soft dough. Spoon the mixture into the greased bread tin and cover lightly with foil. Bake at 375°F, Gas 5, 190°C for 1 hour. Turn out to cool on a wire tray.

Spicy Rolls

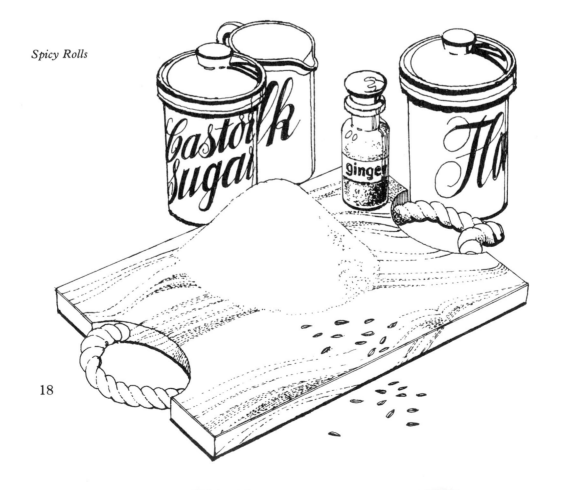

18

Bran Loaf

125 g (5 oz) self-raising flour
50 g (2 oz) bran
100 g (4 oz) caster sugar
pinch of salt
125 g (5 oz) sultanas
milk to mix

Mix all the dry ingredients and add the sultanas. Mix with milk to a soft dough. Put into a greased 1 lb loaf tin and bake at 350°F, Gas 4, 180°C for approximately 1 hour.

Quick Bread

200 g (8 oz) plain flour
200 g (8 oz) wholemeal flour
5 ml (1 teaspoon) cream of tartar
5 ml (1 teaspoon) bicarbonate of soda
25 g (1 oz) caster sugar
5 ml (1 teaspoon) salt
milk and water mixed

Blend dry ingredients well and make a soft dough with the liquid. Turn on to a floured board and knead well until smooth. If the mixture is too soft at this stage extra flour may be kneaded in. Butter a 2 lb bread tin and put the loaf into this. Bake at 400°F, Gas 6, 200°C for 45 minutes. Alternatively, this may be rolled into small rolls and put side by side in a buttered roasting tin to make small bread rolls. These will take 15–20 minutes in the same temperature of oven.

Muffins

25 g (1 oz) butter
250 g (8 oz) flour
2.5 ml (½ teaspoon) salt
25 g (1 oz) baking powder
150 ml (6 fl oz) milk

Rub butter into the dry ingredients. Add milk gradually to form a soft dough. Roll out on a floured board to ½ inch thick and cut into 2 inch rounds. Bake in a hot oven (400°F, Gas 6, 200°C) for 10–15 minutes. Makes 1 dozen.

Boiled Fruit Loaf

125 g (5 oz) soft brown sugar
150 g (6 oz) raisins
50 g (2 oz) mixed peel
10 ml (2 teaspoons) mixed spice
10 ml (2 teaspoons) ground ginger
5 ml (1 teaspoon) cinnamon
pinch salt
125 ml (5 fl oz) water
5 ml (1 teaspoon) bicarbonate of soda
100 g (4 oz) flour
100 g (4 oz) self raising flour

Put all the ingredients except the flours into a large pan and bring to the boil. Keep on the heat, simmering, for about 3 minutes. Sift in the flours and mix well. Put in a greased and lined 2 lb loaf tin and bake at 350°F, Gas 4, 180°C for about 1 hour or until done.

Tea Loaf

200 g (8 oz) mixed dried fruits
100 g (4 oz) soft brown sugar
125 ml (4 fl oz) warm tea
200 g (8 oz) self-raising flour
5 ml (1 teaspoon) mixed spice
15 ml (1 tablespoon) marmalade
1 egg

Soak the fruit and sugar in the tea overnight. Mix in the rest of the ingredients and put into a greased and floured loaf tin. Bake at 350°F, Gas 4, 180°C for 1 hour. *Illustrated in colour between pages 40 and 41.*

Butteries

15 g (½ oz) fresh yeast
15 ml (3 teaspoons) sugar
100 ml (4 fl oz) warm water
5 ml (1 teaspoon) salt
300 g (12 oz) plain flour
75 g (3 oz) lard
75 g (3 oz) margarine

Cream yeast and add 5 ml (1 teaspoon) of the sugar. Add water and leave to froth up. Mix with the salt and flour to make a dough and leave for 1 hour in a warm place. Knead on a floured board. Roll out. Mix the lard and margarine and the rest of the sugar. Spread ⅓ of this over ⅔ of the rolled out dough and fold up like an envelope. Half turn and roll out and repeat the process with another ⅓ of the dough. Repeat once more until the fat is used up. Cut off in pieces. Fold the corners under and put on a greased tray. Set in a warm place to rise for ½ hour. On top of each one place a tiny piece of butter and bake in a hot oven (425°F, Gas 7, 220°C) until crisp. Makes approximately 18.

Date Walnut Loaf

400 g (1 lb) flour
75 g (3 oz) sugar
75 g (3 oz) walnuts
2.5 ml (½ teaspoon) salt
60 ml (4 teaspoons) baking powder
75 g (3 oz) dates
1 egg
milk

Mix the dry ingredients and add the fruit and beaten egg. Add enough milk to form a soft dough. Bake in a greased and floured 2 lb loaf tin, for 1 hour at 350°F, Gas 4, 180°C. *Illustrated in colour between pages 40 and 41.*

Buttery Rolls

500 g (1 lb) plain flour
5 ml (1 teaspoon) bicarbonate of soda
5 ml (1 teaspoon) cream of tartar
5 ml (1 teaspoon) salt
75 g (3 oz) butter
1 egg
200 ml (7 fl oz) milk

Mix dry ingredients in a bowl and rub in the butter. Whisk egg and milk lightly together and add most of this to the dry mixture. Turn on to a floured board and knead lightly. Make up into twists and rings or use a plain cutter. Brush with the rest of the egg and milk mixture and bake in a hot oven (400°F, Gas 6, 200°C) for 20 minutes or until browned.

Walnut Loaf

200 g (8 oz) flour
2.5 ml (½ teaspoon) salt
10 ml (2 teaspoons) baking powder
75 g (3 oz) walnuts
50 g (2 oz) raisins
1 egg
75 g (3 oz) soft brown sugar
200 ml (6 fl oz) milk

Sift the dry ingredients and add the chopped nuts and fruits. Beat the egg and add to the sugar. Stir it in. Add the flour mix alternately with the milk to the egg and sugar. Pour into a lined and greased loaf tin. Stand for 20 minutes and then put into a moderate oven (350°F, Gas 4, 180°C) for an hour. Turn out and eat fresh.

Nut Bread

200 g (8 oz) self raising flour
2.5 ml (½ teaspoon) salt
25 g (1 oz) sugar
25 g (1 oz) chopped nuts
50 g (2 oz) sultanas
1 egg
125 ml (5 fl oz) milk

Sift the dry ingredients and add the sugar, nuts and fruit. Beat the egg in a bowl with the milk and mix into the dry ingredients. Place in a greased and floured 1 lb tin. Bake at 350°F, Gas 4, 180°C for 1 hour.

Currant Loaf

200 g (8 oz) self raising flour
pinch of salt
50 g (2 oz) sugar
100 g (4 oz) currants
1 egg
125 ml (5 fl oz) milk

Mix the dry ingredients. Bind to a soft dough with the egg and some milk as needed. Grease a 1 lb loaf tin and put the mix in this. Bake at 375°F, Gas 5, 190°C for 45 minutes to an hour. Turn out to cool and eat as fresh as possible.

Raisin Bread

250 g (10 oz) wholemeal flour
300 g (12 oz) flour
7.5 ml (1¼ teaspoons) salt
100 g (4 oz) sugar
15 ml (3 teaspoons) baking powder
150 g (6 oz) raisins
1 egg
300 ml (9 fl oz) milk

Mix all the dry ingredients thoroughly. Add the raisins. Beat the egg with the milk and add to form a dough. A little extra milk may be needed to make the dough a soft consistency. Put in a greased 2 lb loaf tin and bake for 45 minutes at 350°F, Gas 4, 180°C or until done. Cool on a wire tray and serve very fresh.

Banana Bread

100 g (4 oz) wholemeal flour
100 g (4 oz) plain flour
10 ml (2 tablespoons) baking powder
pinch of salt
50 g (2 oz) margarine
50 g (2 oz) Barbados sugar
75 g (5 oz) honey
50 g (2 oz) walnuts
1 egg
2 bananas

Sift flours and baking powder and salt. Melt the margarine, sugar and honey. Chop nuts finely and beat the egg in a small bowl. Mash the bananas. Stir the margarine mix into the flours and mix well. Add the rest of the ingredients and stir thoroughly. Bake in a greased and lined 1 lb loaf tin for 1 hour at 350°F, Gas 4, 180°C.

Pastry

As with so many areas of cookery, the plainer the recipe the harder it is to achieve success. This, of course, is because one cannot cover up errors in the plain, but a bit of embroidery on the fancy goes unnoticed! Pastry is no exception and a good plain shortcrust can be difficult to make. So in this section, as well as some basic pastry recipes, I have given recipes for richer and more varied pastries which are much easier to make and which give excellent results. Pâte brisée is lovely if you can make it, but simpler are German pastry and rich short pastry. They are certainly worth trying, for many pastry recipes are interchangeable. Melt-in-the-mouth pastry is wonderful for both sweet and savoury versions.

General rules for pastries are to keep ingredients cool, and to rub in fat very lightly. When adding liquid only, add just enough to bind and only mix this until it is a loose ball. Do not knead too much. Excess liquid and too much kneading will make the pastry tough. It is worth chilling the pastry before using and better still, after lining a flan tin, chill again and this should help to prevent the pastry from shrinking. If you are adding a cooked filling to your flan, bake the pastry 'blind' by setting in the case a sheet of greaseproof paper weighted down with baking beans or rice (which can be kept in a jar for this purpose). Usually, 10–15 minutes will suffice, and then the paper and beans may be lifted out, the filling added and the cooking completed.

BASIC PASTRY RECIPES

Quick Pastry

100 g (4 oz) soft margarine
15 ml (1 tablespoon) water
150 g (6 oz) plain flour

Mix the margarine, water and 2 tablespoons of the flour with a fork. Do not use a mixer. Add the rest of the flour and knead lightly until it is a smooth paste. Roll out and use to line a 7-inch flan case. Suitable for family jam tarts.

Rich Short Pastry

200 g (8 oz) butter
4 egg yolks
1 egg white
200 g (8 oz) sugar
pinch of salt
rind of 1 lemon
350 g (14 oz) flour

Soften the butter to a point where you can stir it easily with a wooden spoon, but not until it is runny. Mix with the egg yolks and white, sugar, salt and rind. Pour this mixture into the centre of a well in the sifted flour. Work in from the centre until all the flour is incorporated. Stand for one hour in the fridge before using to line a tin for flans, tarts etc. Good for jam tart or mince pies.

Pâte Brisée

200 g (8 oz) flour
1 ml (¼ teaspoon) salt
75 g (3 oz) butter
25 g (1 oz) lard or white fat
45 ml (3 tablespoons) iced water

Mix the flour and salt and cut the fats into very small pieces. Put into the flour and chop in with a broad-bladed knife until as fine as possible. Add the water and toss until the liquid is absorbed. Form the dough into a ball and knead lightly with the heel of the hand until the flour is all distributed through the dough. Form into a ball and wrap in greaseproof paper. Chill for at least half an hour and preferably longer.

Rough Puff Pastry

200 g (8 oz) flour
salt
cold water
150 g (6 oz) margarine and white fat mixed
lemon juice

Sift flour and salt and cut in the fat using a broad-bladed knife. Mix to an elastic dough with lemon juice and cold water. Knead lightly on a floured board and roll out in a long strip. Fold in three, seal the ends and half turn. Roll out and repeat again. Chill for 30 minutes and repeat twice more before using the pastry. Bake at

425°F, Gas 7, 220°C until set, and then lower the heat to cook through.

Sweet Flan Pastry

500 g (1 lb) flour
300 g (10 oz) margarine
50 g (2 oz) sugar
2.5 ml (½ teaspoon) salt
5 ml (1 teaspoon) baking powder
2 eggs

Sift the flour and rub in the fat. Add the sugar and the rest of the dry ingredients. Bind with the beaten eggs. Flour a board and roll out the pastry. This quantity will line two 9-inch flans or one large flan and 12 patty tins.

Wholemeal Shortcrust

200 g (8 oz) wholemeal flour
50 g (2 oz) plain white flour
salt
10 ml (2 teaspoons) baking powder
50 g (2 oz) margarine
30 ml (2 tablespoons) cold water

Sift the flours, salt and baking powder together. Rub the fat in lightly and bind with some cold water to form a stiff dough. Roll out on a floured board and use to line two 6-inch tins or one 9-inch tin. Bake blind for 10 minutes or until pastry is set, at 375°F, Gas 6, 200°C.

Melt-in-the-Mouth Pastry

400 g (1 lb) self-raising flour
200 g (8 oz) margarine
100 g (4 oz) white cooking fat
¼ teacup sugar
boiling water

Sift 300 g (12 oz) flour into a bowl. Cut in the margarine and the white fat. Top up the cup in which you have the sugar with boiling water. Stir until the sugar is dissolved and add to the flour mix. Stir and blend with a fork until the fat is well incorporated. Add the last of the flour and mix it in. Roll in greaseproof paper and chill. Use as required.

Flaky Pastry

200 g (8 oz) flour
salt
150 g (6 oz) margarine
lemon juice
cold water

Sift flour and salt and rub in a quarter of the fat. Mix to an elastic dough with lemon juice and water. Turn on to a floured board and knead lightly. Roll out into a long strip. Divide the rest of the fat into three portions. Put one part in small pieces over the surface of two-thirds of the pastry. Fold the plain third in and fold again, forming an envelope. Seal the ends and half turn the pastry. Roll out using short sharp strokes. Do this operation twice

more to use up all the fat. Cool and stand for 30 minutes. Roll and fold once more before using for the tops of pies etc.

Cheese Pastry

50 g (2 oz) cheese
100 g (4 oz) flour
pinch each of salt, pepper and dry mustard
75 g (3 oz) butter
egg to bind

Grate the cheese finely. Sift flour, salt, pepper and mustard and then rub in the butter. Add the cheese and combine with enough egg to form a stiff dough. Roll out on a floured board and line flan tins, or patty tins and fill as desired. Excellent for savoury dishes.

Choux Pastry

150 ml (6 fl oz) water
50 g (2 oz) butter
75 g (3 oz) flour
salt
2 eggs

Bring water and butter to a boil and add the sifted flour and salt. Stir until a smooth ball is formed. Cool slightly and beat in the eggs one at a time. Beat well. Put the mixture into a large forcing bag with a fairly wide plain nozzle. Pipe on to a greased baking sheet in fingers or in bun shapes. Bake at 400°F, Gas 6, 200°C until pale brown and firm. Cool, split and remove any uncooked dough in the middle. Fill with whipped sweetened cream and ice as desired. These may also be used with savoury fillings.

German Pastry

125 g (5 oz) butter or margarine
100 g (4 oz) caster sugar
1 egg yolk
200 g (8 oz) flour

Cream the fat and sugar. Add yolk and work in flour. Chill for 30 minutes before using and do not roll it out too thinly or it will be tricky to handle. Use for fruit squares, apple tarts etc.

Oatmeal Pastry

100 g (4 oz) flour
100 g (4 oz) oatmeal

salt
50 g (2 oz) butter
cold water

Mix flour, meal and salt. Rub in the butter and bind with just enough water to make a firm paste. Roll out and use to line flan tins for dishes such as leek and cheese pie, or egg and bacon with spinach.

Biscuit Crust

200 g (8 oz) margarine and cooking fat mixed
50 g (2 oz) caster sugar
1 egg yolk
salt
300 g (12 oz) flour

Cream fat and sugar and add the yolk, salt and flour to form a stiff paste. Chill before using to line tart or flan tins. This may be made by the all-in-one method in a mixer.

SWEET PASTRY DISHES
Romaine's Delicious Chocolate Pie

Pastry

125 g (5 oz) margarine
200 g (8 oz) flour
25 g (1 oz) sugar
2.5 ml (½ teaspoon) baking powder
1 egg

Filling

125 g (5 oz) chocolate
25 g (1 oz) butter
3 egg whites
75 g (3 oz) sugar
75 g (3 oz) browned ground almonds

Rub the fat into the flour and add the sugar and baking powder. Bind with an egg and use to line two 8 inch fluted flan rings. Line with greaseproof paper and fill with baking beans or rice. Bake blind for 15 minutes at 375°F, Gas 5, 190°C. Remove the paper and the beans and continue to bake for a further 5 to 10 minutes until firm and browned. Cool. One case may be frozen for future use, or wrapped in foil or stored in an airtight tin for 2–3 days. This pastry is very easy to handle and freezes well.

Filling: melt the chocolate and butter in a double boiler. Beat the egg whites until stiff and add the sugar. Beat again until stiff. Add the almonds to the chocolate mix and fold in the whites using a balloon whisk. Pour into the pastry case and bake in a moderate oven (350°F, Gas 4, 180°C) for 25 minutes. Serve hot with cream.

Fruit Squares

Filling

100 g (4 oz) margarine
100 g (4 oz) flour
½ kilo (1 lb) mixed dried fruit
50 g (2 oz) sugar
3 stewed apples

Fruit Squares

28

Pastry

25 g (1 oz) butter
½ kilo (1 lb) flour
50 g (2 oz) sugar
2.5 ml (½ teaspoon) salt
5 ml (1 teaspoon) baking powder
3 eggs, lightly beaten

Melt the margarine for the filling and stir the flour into the fruits with the sugar. Bind with the apple and the margarine. Cool. For the pastry, rub the butter into the flour and add the rest of the dry ingredients and blend well. Bind with the eggs. Knead lightly on a floured board and use half the pastry to line a square tin approximately 8 inches by 8 inches by 2 inches. Fill the mixed fruits into this and top with the rest of the pastry. This pastry tends to be crumbly but does not mind being pushed into corners and used for patching holes. Brush the top with egg and sprinkle with caster sugar. Bake at 375°F, Gas 5, 190°C for 35 to 40 minutes. Cool in the tin to serve for tea or else serve hot with cream as a pudding.

Yum-yum Bars

Pastry

50 g (2 oz) soft brown sugar
75 g (3 oz) margarine
2 egg yolks
5 ml (1 teaspoon) vanilla essence
150 g (6 oz) self raising flour

Topping

2 egg whites
100 g (4 oz) caster sugar
25 g (1 oz) chopped glacé cherries
25 g (1 oz) chopped nuts

Cream sugar and margarine and then beat in the yolks. Add the essence and flour and make into a stiff paste. Grease a swiss roll tin and press the mixture into this. Beat the egg white until stiff and add the sugar, fruit and nuts. Fold them in lightly and spread over the top of the pastry. Bake at 350°F, Gas 4, 180°C for 30 minutes. Cool in the tray and then mark into fingers. Makes about 18.

Almond Buns

Pastry

150 g (6 oz) flour
pinch of salt
2.5 ml (½ teaspoon) baking powder
75 g (3 oz) margarine
1 egg
50 g (2 oz) caster sugar

Filling

50 g (2 oz) ground almonds
25 g (1 oz) caster sugar
25 g (1 oz) icing sugar
almond essence
little grated orange rind
egg to bind
few nibbed almonds

Sift the flour, salt and baking powder together. Cut and rub in the margarine and bind with egg. Stir in the sugar. Mix all the filling ingredients together to form a paste. Divide the pastry into 16 pieces. Do the same with the paste. Using the heel of the hand flatten the pastry, top with a piece of paste, and fold over. Seal and place upside down on a greased baking sheet. Brush with remaining egg and sprinkle with nibbed almonds. Bake at 425°F, Gas 7, 220°C for 15 minutes. *Illustrated in colour opposite page 40.*

Walnut and Whisky Orange Flan

100 g (4 oz) rich short pastry (page 24)
75 g (3 oz) sugar
75 g (3 oz) butter
2 eggs, separated
50 g (2 oz) raisins
15 ml (1 tablespoon) whisky
25 g (1 oz) chopped walnuts
2 oranges, peeled and chopped
25 g (1 oz) plain flour
50 g (2 oz) rice flour
6 unbroken half walnuts

Line an 8-inch flan ring with the pastry and bake blind for 15 minutes. Remove from the oven. Beat the sugar and butter lightly and add the egg yolks. Simmer the raisins in the whisky for 1 minute. Put them, the chopped nuts and the oranges into the half-cooked flan case. Beat the egg whites until stiff, and fold into the butter mix with the flour and rice flour sifted together. Spread on top of the fruit. Arrange the half walnuts on top, and bake in a moderately hot oven (375°F, Gas 5, 190°C) for 15 minutes.

Apple Tarts

200 g (8 oz) melt-in-the-mouth pastry (page 26)
1 cup apple purée, flavoured with cinnamon or cloves
whole almonds
milk
sugar

Roll out the pastry and cut in rounds enough to line and top 2 inch patty tins. Line the tins, half fill with the well-flavoured apple purée and slip in a whole almond. Brush edges with a little milk and put the tops in place. Brush lightly with a little more milk and sprinkle with caster sugar. Bake at 400°F, Gas 6, 200°C for 15 minutes. *Illustrated in colour opposite page 40.*

Caramel Tart

200 g (8 oz) rich short pastry (page 24)
150 g (6 oz) soft brown sugar
75 g (3 oz) margarine
20 ml (2 dessertspoons) cornflour
a little cold water
a cup of hot water
1 ml (¼ teaspoon) vanilla essence
2 egg whites
100 g (4 oz) caster sugar

Line a 9-inch tart tin with the pastry and bake it blind. Melt the sugar and margarine. Mix the cornflour to a paste with a little cold water and add a cup of boiling water. Stir in with the caramel mix and boil until it thickens. Flavour with the vanilla. Whisk the egg whites until very stiff, then whisk in the caster sugar. Fill the caramel mix into the pastry shell and top with the meringue. Put into a very hot oven (450°F, Gas 8, 225°C) for a few minutes to brown the meringue. Serve hot.

Sift the flour and rub in the fat. Add the sugar and almond essence. Mix in enough water to bind. Roll out and use to line a greased 7 inch tart tin. Mix all the filling ingredients to a thick cream and pour into the tart case. Bake at 400°F, Gas 6, 200°C for 12 to 15 minutes. Two minutes before the end sprinkle with sugar.

Almond Tart

Pastry

100 g (4 oz) flour
50 g (2 oz) butter
25 g (1 oz) sugar
2 ml (½ teaspoon) almond essence
water to bind

Filling

2 eggs
75 g (3 oz) sugar
75 g (3 oz) ground almonds
small glass of milk

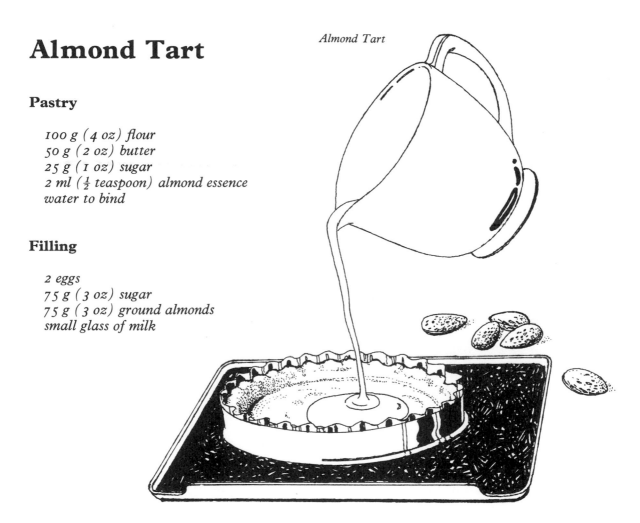

Almond Tart

Syrup Tart

100 g (4 oz) rich short pastry (page 24)
125 g (6 oz) syrup
50 g (2 oz) fresh white bread crumbs
lemon juice

Line a 6-inch flan ring with the pastry. Keep trimmings for decoration. Warm syrup in a small pan and add fresh white bread crumbs. Add lemon juice to take the sweetness out and fill the mix into the pastry case. Bake at 400°F, Gas 6, 200°C for 30 minutes.

Nut Rolls

rough puff pastry (page 25)
finely-chopped walnuts
redcurrant jelly
egg white
caster sugar

Roll out the pastry to a quarter inch thick. Mix the finely-chopped nuts with some red-current jelly to form a stiff paste. Cut the pastry into 2 inch wide strips and spread with the nut mix. Roll up and brush with the beaten egg white. Sprinkle with sugar and bake in a hot oven 425°F, Gas 7, 220°C until brown.

Nut Rolls

32

Open Apple Tart

200 g (8 oz) pâte brisée (page 25)
cooking apples
25 g (1 oz) demerara sugar
1 ml (¼ teaspoon) cinnamon
25 g (1 oz) demerara sugar
grated rind of 1 lemon
½ cup sponge cake crumbs

Line a flan tin with the pâte brisée. Peel, core and slice apples and arrange in overlapping circles in the flan case to give a reasonable depth of fruit. Sprinkle with the cinnamon and sugar, and add the lemon rind. Mix the cake crumbs and the rest of the sugar and cover the apples with this mix. Dot with butter and bake in a moderately hot oven (400°F, Gas 6, 200°C) until the pastry is cooked, about 30 minutes.

Coconut Macaroon Pie

150 g (6 oz) melt-in-the-mouth pastry
(page 26)
2 eggs
200 g (8 oz) caster sugar
100 g (4 oz) butter
35 g (1½ oz) flour
100 ml (3 fl oz) milk
75 g (3 oz) coconut

Line a deep 9-inch flan tin with the pastry. Bake the shell blind. Beat the eggs and add the sugar. Beat well until smooth and lemon coloured. Soften the butter and beat it in to the sugar mix. Add the flour and the milk and beat well. Stir in the coconut and pour the mix into the pie shell. Bake at 325°F, Gas 3, 160°C for 1 hour. If you cannot obtain a deep flan tin this quantity will do two small ones, in which case take 5 to 10 minutes off the cooking time.

Strawberry Cream Pie

200 g (8 oz) melt-in-the-mouth pastry
(page 26)
75 g (3 oz) white marshmallows
15 g (½ oz) gelatine
30 ml (2 tablespoons) water
juice of half a lemon
300 ml (½ pint) cream
2 egg whites
50 g (2 oz) caster sugar
½ kilo (1 lb) washed and hulled
strawberries

Make the pastry into a 9-inch flan case and cool. Snip the marshmallows into quarters using wet scissors (this stops them sticking). Melt the gelatine in water and juice by adding it to the cold liquid and very gently warming until the mixture lightly stings the end of the finger. Beat the cream and egg whites together. Using a balloon whisk add the gelatine to the cream mix, and then fold in the marshmallows and strawberries, reserving a few for the top. Pour into the pastry shell and decorate.

Lemon Meringue Pie

7-inch baked biscuit crust shell (page 27)
25 g (1 oz) sugar
juice and grated rind of one lemon
25 g (1 oz) butter
125 ml (4 fl oz) water
25 g (1 oz) cornflour
1 egg, separated
pinch of salt
50 g (2 oz) sugar for meringue

Make a sauce by combining the sugar with the lemon juice, rind, butter, water and cornflour. Check for sweetening and add sugar if needed. Cool a little and add the egg yolk. Pour into the shell. Make a meringue by beating the white stiff with the salt and folding the sugar in with a wire whisk. Place on top of the lemon filling and make sure it is taken well to the edges. Bake at 325°F, Gas 3, 160°C for 20 minutes.

Border Tart

150 g (4 oz) rich short pastry (page 24)
50 g (2 oz) margarine
50 g (2 oz) caster sugar
1 egg
1 cup mixed dried fruit
1 ml (¼ teaspoon) baking powder
1 ml (¼ teaspoon) vanilla

Line a 7-inch flan ring with pastry. Keep the trimmings for decoration. Cream the fat and sugar until light and add the egg, fruit and baking powder with the vanilla. Put into the case and decorate with the pastry cut in strips to form a lattice. Bake for 5 minutes at 400°F, Gas 6, 200°C and a further 25 to 30 minutes at 350°F, Gas 4, 180°C.

Raisin Tart

300 g (12 oz) melt-in-the-mouth pastry
  (page 26)
75 g (3 oz) margarine
225 g (9 oz) caster sugar
3 eggs
200 g (8 oz) raisins
5 ml (1 teaspoon) vanilla essence

Line a swiss roll tin with the pastry. Cream the margarine and sugar and when creamy beat in the eggs. Mix in the raisins and essence. Bake at 350°F, Gas 4, 180°C for 30 to 40 minutes. When cool cut into fingers. Makes about 24.

Macaroon Cakes

50 g (2 oz) lard
50 g (2 oz) butter
200 g (8 oz) self raising flour
5 ml (1 teaspoon) caster sugar
milk

Filling

2 egg whites
150 g (6 oz) caster sugar
75 g (3 oz) coconut

Rub the fats into the flour and add the sugar. Bind to a stiff paste with a little milk. Roll out thinly and use to line 18 patty tins. Beat the egg whites until stiff and then beat in the sugar. Fold in the coconut. Fill the uncooked patty cases and bake in a moderate oven 350°F, Gas 4, 180°C for 15 minutes.

Fresh Fruit Bakewell Tart

200 g (8 oz) rich short pastry (page 24)
½ kilo (1 lb) fresh stewed apple, pear,
  gooseberry or plums
50 g (2 oz) butter
50 g (2 oz) caster sugar
1 egg
50 g (2 oz) ground almonds

Line a flan tin with the pastry and fill with the fruit, straining off as much of the juice as possible. Cream the butter and sugar and stir in the egg. Beat again and fold in the almonds. Bake in a hot oven (400°F, Gas 6, 200°C) for about 15 minutes.

Strawberry Flan

200 g (8 oz) pâte brisée (page 25)
½ kilo (1 lb) strawberries
sugar
5 ml (1 teaspoon) lemon juice
1 small carton double cream
5 ml (1 teaspoon) arrowroot

Make an 8-inch flan shell with the pâte brisée and cook blind. Wash and hull the strawberries and arrange the best of them in the pastry case. Crush the rest and sweeten to taste. Cook gently until soft and juicy. Add the lemon juice and sieve the resultant purée. Make up to half a pint with water if required. Blend the arrowroot with a little cold water and add to the strawberry mix. Cook until thick and pour over the flan. Cool and decorate with piped whipped cream.

SAVOURY PASTRY DISHES

Hunt Pie

1 oz dripping
1 onion
100 g (4 oz) mince
50 g (2 oz) brown lentils
2 carrots
piece turnip
1 stick celery
1 cup stock
seasoning
200 g (8 oz) rough puff pastry (page 25)

Melt dripping and sauté onion and mince in it until brown. Add lentils and vegetables suitably cut in dice. Add stock and season with salt and pepper. Pour into a lightly greased pie dish with pie funnel. Top with rough puff pastry. Trim edges and make leaf shapes for garnishing the top. Make three or four small slits for the steam to escape and brush lightly with egg or milk. Bake for 45 minutes in a moderately hot oven (400°F, Gas 6, 200°C).

Mince Tart

½ kilo (1 lb) rough puff pastry (page 25)
1 onion
200 g (8 oz) mince
2 tomatoes
50 g (2 oz) porridge oats
salt and pepper to taste
½ cup stock

Line a pie plate with half the pastry. Cook onion, mince and tomato together until browned. Add oats, seasoning and stock if needed. Fill into the pastry and cover with the rest of the pastry. Trim. Knock up the edges with a knife. Decorate and brush with beaten egg. Cook for 45 minutes at 400°F, Gas 6, 200°C. Serve hot.

Kipper Flan

6-inch half-baked wholemeal shortcrust (page 25)
73 g (3 oz) cooked kipper
2 chopped hard boiled eggs
½ cup (1 gill) white sauce, flavoured with bay and mace

Flake the fish and mix with the chopped eggs. Fold into the white sauce and fill into the flan case. Bake at 350°F, Gas 4, 180°C for 30 minutes or until cooked.

Cheese Tart

200 g (8 oz) oatmeal pastry (page 27)
125 g (5 oz) grated cheese
2 eggs
1 cup milk
salt and pepper

Line a 7-inch flan with the pastry. Mix the grated cheese with the beaten eggs. Bring milk to the boil and pour onto the cheese mix. Season and pour into flan case. Bake for 25 to 30 minutes in a moderately hot oven (375°F, Gas 5, 190°C). Alternatively bake in patty tins, in which case the baking time will be only 15 to 20 minutes.

Mushroom Turnovers

Pastry

300 g (12 oz) flour
250 g (10 oz) butter
5 ml (1 teaspoon) salt
60 ml (2 fluid ounces) iced water

Filling

200 g (8 oz) mushrooms
cup water
3 spring onions
25 g (1 oz) butter
2 tablespoons parsley
15 ml (1 tablespoon) lemon juice
10 ml (½ teaspoon) salt
1 ml (¼ teaspoon) tabasco
25 g (1 oz) butter
25 g (1 oz) flour
½ cup sour cream

Sift flour and make a well. Add butter, water and salt. Cut in with a broad bladed knife at first and then work with cool hands into a smooth paste. Wrap and chill for one hour.

Simmer the stalks of the mushrooms in a cup of water and a pinch of salt. Keep the broth. Sauté the chopped spring onions in the melted butter and add the parsley, juice, salt and tabasco. Add the wiped mushroom caps and cook with a lid on for

3 to 5 minutes. Blend the butter and flour and add half a cup of the mushroom stock. Cook until the flour bursts. Stir in the sour cream and mix it in with the mushrooms. Cut the pastry into large rounds. Put a spoonful of the mushroom mix in the middle of each. Moisten the edges and fold over. Seal. Brush the tops with beaten egg and bake at 400°F, Gas 6, 200°C for 15 minutes. Serve hot.

Forfar Bridies

½ kilo (1 lb) rough puff pastry (page 25)
½ kilo (1 lb) good steak
75 g (3 oz) minced suet
1 small chopped onion

Divide pastry in three and roll out to large thin ovals. Cut the meat into very fine thin strips and add a seasoning of salt and pepper. Divide between the ovals of pastry. Put on each a part of the suet and some onion. Brush the edges with water and fold over to make into a semicircle. Seal the edges and trim as needed. Brush with egg or milk and start cooking in a hot oven (450°F, Gas 8, 225°C) and when pastry is set reduce to 350°F, Gas 4, 180°C and cook until meat is tender.

Bacon and Onion Flan

6 inch baked wholemeal shortcrust (page 25)
100 g (4 oz) streaky bacon

1 large onion
1 egg
30 ml (2 tablespoons) cream
black pepper

Chop the bacon and sauté gently in a heavy skillet until the fat runs well. Peel and chop the onion finely and add to the bacon. Continue to cook gently till crisp and the onion is transparent. Mix the egg and cream with a fork and season with freshly ground black pepper. Drain the onion and bacon of as much fat as possible and put into the flan case. Pour the egg and cream mix over the top and bake in a moderate oven (350°F, Gas 4, 180°C) for 30 minutes. Serve hot or cold.

Marjoram Flavoured Mushroom Tarts

4 cooked individual tart-size pastry cases
100 g (4 oz) streaky bacon
200 g (8 oz) mushrooms, washed and
*   sliced*
salt
black pepper
15 ml (1 tablespoon) fresh marjoram
small carton cream

Chop the bacon finely and put over a gentle heat in a heavy sauté pan. When the fat runs, add the mushrooms. Cook until tender. Add a very small pinch of salt if required, plenty of freshly ground black pepper, the marjoram very finely minced and finally the cream. Reheat to thicken the cream and fill into the pastry cases. Serve at once.

Honey & Oats

Honey is one ingredient in cookery which requires a little care. It has a tendency to burn if not very carefully watched and you will note that the recipes which include it are on the whole cooked in not too hot an oven. The cakes included are all lovely, and can be varied by using different flavoured honeys. For instance, a cake made with a strong-flavoured honey like acacia or heather will taste quite different from one made with a mixed-flower honey. You can, of course, suit your requirements in this direction to your personal taste. Honey may also be used instead of sugar in a number of recipes providing a reduction is made in the amount of liquid added to the cake. For instance 100 g (4 oz) sugar can be replaced by $\frac{3}{4}$ cup of honey and $\frac{1}{4}$ of the other liquids left out. I have taken a standard 6 fluid ounce cup as being the cup measure used.

Most people will think of porridge or oatcakes when they think of oats, but it is also used in such things as haggis, mealy puddings, stuffings, and not surprisingly in baking of various kinds. Oats themselves are ground into assorted grades, but for baking I have found that the ordinary medium oatmeal does very well. Included also in this section are some recipes using Porage oats, or what in England are called rolled oats. These, being partly cooked, have a great number of uses from the usual porridge to stuffing or meat loaf. The baking recipes are all for sweet things but the oatmeal pastry in the pastry section can be used with success for a number of savoury pies. Oats may be used very nicely to give crunch to many otherwise soft mixtures, and give a nice contrast to fruit fillings.

Fruit Honey Cake

100 g (4 oz) candied lemon peel
100 g (4 oz) orange peel
100 g (4 oz) citron
600 g (1½ lb) mixed glacé fruits (e.g. pineapple, figs, peaches etc.)
200 g (8 oz) raisins
100 ml (6 tablespoons) pineapple juice
75 g (3 oz) roasted hazelnuts
50 g (2 oz) split almonds
50 g (2 oz) walnuts
300 g (12 oz) flour
100 g (4 oz) butter
100 g (4 oz) sugar
½ cup honey
5 eggs
5 ml (1 teaspoon) salt
5 ml (1 teaspoon) baking powder
allspice
cloves

Prepare the fruits by cutting the peels into small pieces. Scissors are the best implement for this. Chop the glacé fruits and leave them and the peels to soak overnight in the pineapple juice. The following day add the chopped nuts and two tablespoons of the sifted flour. Cream butter and sugar well together and add the honey gradually. Add eggs one at a time, beating all the time. Add flour, salt, baking powder and sifted spices and beat in. Add fruits and nuts mixture and blend thoroughly. Line two 9-inch by 5-inch by 2-inch cake tins or charlotte tins. Decorate the base with glacé cherries and almonds and fill in the mixture. Bake at 275°F, Gas 1, 140°C for 3½ to 4 hours. Keep a small dish of water in the oven to stop drying out. Cool and wrap in a sherry soaked muslin and foil and store for 3 to 4 weeks before using. *Illustrated in colour opposite page 41.*

40

Almond Buns (front) and Apple Tarts

Gingerbread and, on board, Tea Loaf (right) and Date Walnut Loaf

Honey Spice Cake (left) and Fruit Honey Cake

Traditional Honey Cake

6 eggs
150 g (6 oz) sugar
150 ml (6 fl oz) honey
30 ml (2 tablespoons) oil
325 g (14 oz) flour
8 ml (1½ teaspoons) baking soda
1 ml (¼ teaspoon) ground cloves
1 ml (¼ teaspoon) cinnamon
85 g (3 oz) raisins
50 g (2 oz) chopped walnuts
25 g (1 oz) citron peel
30 ml (2 tablespoons) whisky

Whisk eggs and gradually add the sugar. Beat until very light and fluffy. Fold in the oil, honey and the sifted dry ingredients. Add the fruit and whisky with the nuts. Pour into a lined 10-inch square tin and cook at 300°F, Gas 2, 150°C for one hour.

Little Honey Cakes

125 g (5 oz) butter
100 g (4 oz) sugar
300 g (12 oz) flour
10 ml (2 teaspoons) baking powder
5 ml (1 teaspoon) lemon juice
2 eggs
100 g (4 oz) honey
pinch of salt

Grease and flour 24 patty tins. Cream sugar and butter and add the yolks of the eggs. Beat in. Stir in the warmed honey and lemon juice. Stir in the flour, baking powder and salt all sifted together. Whisk the egg whites very stiff and fold in. Half-fill the patty tins and bake in a hot oven (400°F, Gas 6, 200°C) for 10 minutes.

Honey Tart

150 g (6 oz) rich short pastry (page 24)
150 g (6 oz) honey
lemon juice
75 g (3 oz) white breadcrumbs

Line a pie plate with the pastry and keep trimmings. Warm the honey and lemon juice. Stir in the breadcrumbs and pour the mix into the pastry case. Twist the trimmings and lay on top like the spokes of a wheel before baking at 400°F, Gas 6, 200°C for about 30 minutes. Puff pastry may be used if preferred.

Honey Spice Cake

100 g (4 oz) margarine
75 g (3½ oz) caster sugar
100 ml (½ cup) honey
2 eggs
200 g (8 oz) flour
5 ml (1 teaspoon) baking powder
1 ml (¼ teaspoon) bicarbonate of soda
pinch of salt
5 ml (1 teaspoon) cinnamon
1 ml (¼ teaspoon) ground cloves
1 ml (¼ teaspoon) ginger
100 ml (½ cup) water
50 g (2 oz) chopped nuts

Filling

small carton double cream
50 ml (¼ cup) honey

Cream fat and sugar and then add the honey and eggs. Beat for one minute to incorporate well. Stir in the sifted dry ingredients and water. Add nuts and turn into two greased and base-lined sandwich tins. Bake at 350°F, Gas 4, 180°C for 25 to 30 minutes. Allow to rest in the tins for a few minutes before turning out. Cool on a wire tray. Whip the cream and honey together and use to fill and top the cake. Decorate with thin slices of preserved ginger. *Illustrated in colour opposite page 41.*

Honey Almond Biscuits

150 g (6 oz) margarine
30 ml (2 tablespoons) honey
30 ml (2 teaspoons) vanilla essence
175 g (7 oz) flour
25 g (1 oz) icing sugar
75 g (3 oz) almonds

Beat margarine and honey together in a bowl. Add vanilla and fold in flour and icing sugar. Beat until smooth. Chill for an hour. Roll into small balls and put well apart on a greased baking tray. Flatten slightly with a fork, and top with the almonds. Bake for 15 to 20 minutes at 325°F, Gas 3, 160°C. Cool for five minutes before transferring to a wire tray.

Honey Almond Biscuits

42

Honey Fruitcakes

200 g (8 oz) honey
50 g (2 oz) butter
1 egg
200 g (8 oz) flour
50 g (2 oz) currants
2.5 ml (½ teaspoon) baking soda

Heat honey and butter very gently and cook a little. Add beaten egg and flour. Fold in currants and soda. Beat for a minute. Grease a tray of patty tins and half-fill with the mixture. Bake in a moderately hot oven (400°F, Gas 6, 200°C) for 10 to 15 minutes. Watch carefully, for honey burns very quickly.

Honey Spice Squares

150 g (6 oz) honey
50 g (2 oz) sugar
2 eggs plus 1 extra yolk
30 ml (2 tablespoons) cocoa
½ cup (4 fl oz) milk
150 g (6 oz) flour
2.5 ml (½ teaspoon) cinnamon
1 ml (¼ teaspoon) each of cardamom,
  ginger, cloves and baking soda
50 g (2 oz) candied orange peel

Glaze

1 cup icing sugar
30 ml (2 tablespoons) hot water
2.5 ml (½ teaspoon) vanilla essence
glacé cherries to decorate

Beat the honey, sugar and eggs until thick. Stir in cocoa and milk and then fold in the sifted dry ingredients and finely-chopped peel. Spread in a buttered swiss roll tin. Bake at 400°F, Gas 6, 200°C for 12 minutes. Keep warm. Mix ingredients for the glaze and when of a spreading consistency put on top of the bar. Decorate with glacé cherries and cool. Cut in squares allowing a cherry per square. Makes 24.

Honey Cake

½ cup caster sugar
1 cup sour cream
2 cups flour
30 ml (2 tablespoons) honey
2.5 ml (½ teaspoon) bicarbonate of soda

Mix sugar and cream together. Sift flour and add to the cream. Add honey and soda. Beat strongly for 5 minutes and pour into a buttered 6-inch cake tin. Bake in a moderately hot oven (350°F, Gas 4, 180°C) for half to three quarters of an hour.

Oatmeal Gingerbread

125 g (5 oz) flour
175 g (7 oz) oatmeal
5 ml (1 teaspoon) ground ginger
2.5 (½ teaspoon) bicarbonate of soda
2.5 ml (½ teaspoon) cream of tartar
pinch of salt
50 g (2 oz) peel

100 g (4 oz) butter
125 ml (5 fl oz) milk
200 g (8 oz) golden syrup
2 eggs

Mix dry ingredients in a large bowl. Put butter, milk and syrup in a small pan and melt gently. When butter is all melted add the beaten eggs. Make a well in the dry ingredients and add the liquid. Stir well in. Pour into a greased and lined 8-inch cake tin. Bake in a moderate oven for 1½ hours (350°F, Gas 4, 180°C).

Spiced Oatmeal Cake

100 g (4 oz) flour
2.5 ml (½ teaspoon) each of ground
  ginger, cinnamon and sugar
10 g (½ oz) butter
75 g (3 oz) oatmeal
2.5 ml (½ teaspoon) bicarbonate of soda
30 g (2 tablespoons) syrup
30 ml (2 tablespoons) milk
½ egg

Sift flour and spices. Rub in the butter and then add the rest of the dry ingredients. Dissolve the syrup in milk and add the egg. Pour on to the dry ingredients and mix well. Put into a greased and floured 7-inch cake tin. Bake for the first 15 minutes at 400°F, Gas 6, 200°C and then reduce the heat for a further 15 minutes at 350°F, Gas 4, 180°C. Nice with butter.

44

Oatcakes

150 g (6 oz) oatmeal
pinch of bicarbonate of soda
pinch of salt
15 ml (½ oz) lard
hot water

Mix the dry ingredients and add the fat and hot water to make a fairly stiff dough. Roll out thinly on a board sprinkled with oatmeal. Divide into four pieces. Lightly grease a girdle and heat it. When well heated put the oatcakes onto it and cook until the edges curl. Remove from the girdle and set under a hot grill to cook until crisp. Alternatively they can be cooked in a moderate oven (350°F, Gas 4, 180°C) for 10 minutes.

Rich Oatcakes

200 g (8 oz) oatmeal
60 g (1½ oz) flour
25 g (1 oz) sugar
2.5 ml (½ teaspoon) baking powder
1 ml (¼ teaspoon) cream of tartar
2.5 ml (½ teaspoon) salt
75 g (3 oz) margarine or butter
30 ml (2 tablespoons) milk

Mix all dry ingredients in a bowl and rub in fat very lightly. Bind with milk. Roll out on a board sprinkled with oatmeal and cut into large biscuits. Bake on a greased baking sheet for 20 minutes at 325°F, Gas 3, 160°C.

Rolled Oat Shortbread

100 g (4 oz) margarine
50 g (2 oz) demerara sugar
100 g (4 oz) rolled oats
60 g (2½ oz) flour
1 ml (¼ teaspoon) baking soda
pinch of salt

Melt margarine over a low heat and then stir in the rest of ingredients. Spread in a 9-inch by 5-inch greased tin and press down well. Bake for 45 minutes at 400°F, Gas 6, 200°C. When you take it from the oven mark the shortbread into fingers while it is still hot. Leave in the tin to cool thoroughly before removing.

Oaten Shorties

50 g (2 oz) caster sugar
100 g (4 oz) butter
100 g (4 oz) rolled oats
50 g (2 oz) flour

Rub together the butter and sugar and work in the dry ingredients. When the dough is soft and easily handled, roll out on a floured board and cut into fingers approximately 2 inches by 1 inch. Put on a greased baking sheet and bake in a moderate oven (350°F, Gas 4, 180°C) for about 20 minutes. Makes about 18 of this size.

Rolled Oat Shortbread

Spicy Oat Biscuits

100 g (4 oz) margarine
100 g (4 oz) soft brown sugar
100 g (4 oz) rolled oats
100 g (4 oz) self raising flour
1 egg yolk
5 ml (1 teaspoon) cinnamon

Cream margarine and sugar until creamy. Add all dry ingredients and egg yolk. Mix well. Roll out and cut into fingers. Bake at 350°F, Gas 4, 180°C for about 20 minutes until brown. Makes about 18.

Coffee Meal Biscuits

100 g (4 oz) margarine
50 g (2 oz) caster sugar
10 ml (1 dessertspoon) golden syrup
15 g (½ oz) coconut
125 g (5 oz) porridge oats
50 g (2 oz) flour
1 ml (¼ teaspoon) baking powder
1 ml (¼ teaspoon) salt
little coffee-flavoured water icing

Cream margarine and sugar. Beat in syrup and then work in the dry ingredients with a wooden spoon. Roll out on a floured board, but do not roll it too thin. Cut in to small plain rounds and cook on a greased baking sheet in a moderate oven (400°F, Gas 6, 200°C) for about 15 minutes or until golden. Cool on a wire tray and fill with a buttercream flavoured with coffee essence. Top with a little coffee-flavoured water icing.

Oaty Thins

100 g (4 oz) margarine
150 g (6 oz) rolled oats
150 g (6 oz) brown sugar
5 ml (1 teaspoon) baking powder
1 ml (¼ teaspoon) salt
1 egg, beaten

Melt margarine in a small pan. Mix all dry ingredients. Add margarine and egg to the dry ingredients, blend well. Drop in teaspoons on a well-greased baking sheet, leaving 3 inches all round, as they spread during cooking. Bake at 400°F, Gas 6, 200°C until golden brown and lacy. Cool slightly before removing carefully with a broad spatula to a wire tray to cool. Makes 24.

Parkin Biscuits

200 g (8 oz) plain flour
200 g (8 oz) oatmeal
150 g (6 oz) sugar
1 ml (¼ teaspoon) baking powder
5 ml (1 teaspoon) each of ground ginger,
   mixed spice and cinnamon
100 g (4 oz) lard
1 egg
150 g (6 oz) golden syrup
some whole almonds

Mix all dry ingredients well and rub in lard. Beat egg and syrup in a small bowl and add to dry mix. Blend well and form into small balls. Put on a greased baking sheet and press into the middle of each a whole almond, slightly flattening the biscuit at the same time. Bake in a moderate oven (350°F, Gas 4, 180°C) for 20 minutes.

Cream margarine, caster sugar, vanilla essence, syrup and treacle in a bowl. Add water and beat in with mixed dry ingredients. Roll into small balls and flatten slightly on a greased baking sheet. Bake at 350°F, Gas 4, 180°C for 15 to 20 minutes.

Almond Oat Biscuits

100 g (4 oz) margarine
50 g (2 oz) sugar
50 g (2 oz) flour
125 g (5 oz) rolled oats
2.5 ml (½ teaspoon) salt
pinch of baking soda
50 g (2 oz) chopped almonds

Cream fat and sugar and work in dry ingredients. Sprinkle a board with more oats and roll out mixture on this. Cut into biscuits using a plain 1- or 1½-inch cutter. Roughen the surface slightly with a fork to give a nice textured appearance and place on a greased baking sheet. Cook at 400°F, Gas 6, 200°C for 10–15 minutes or until golden.

Golden Crunchies

100 g (4 oz) margarine
5 ml (1 teaspoon) vanilla essence
5 ml (1 teaspoon) each of golden syrup,
*   treacle and warm water*
100 g (4 oz) caster sugar
100 g (4 oz) self raising flour
75 g (3 oz) rolled oats
2.5 ml (½ teaspoon) bicarbonate of soda

Oat Bars

200 g (8 oz) margarine
200 g (8 oz) Barbados or dark brown
*   sugar*
200 g (8 oz) rolled oats
pinch of salt

Melt margarine and sugar and stir in oats and salt. Butter a small swiss roll tin and press the mixture in. Bake at 350°F, Gas 5, 180°C for 15 to 20 minutes until browned. Cut in fingers when cold. Makes about 18 nice sticky bars.

Oatmeal Cheese Biscuits

75 g (3 oz) lard
100 g (4 oz) self-raising flour
100 g (4 oz) oatmeal
pinch of salt
mustard
75 g (3 oz) grated cheese
*   water*

Rub the fat into the flour and oatmeal with the salt and mustard added. Mix in the grated cheese and then add water only if it is needed to form a stiff paste. This will depend on the dryness of the cheese. Roll out and cut into rounds. Bake at 350°F, Gas 4, 180°C for about 20 minutes.

Flapjacks

50 g (2 oz) butter
50 g (2 oz) soft brown sugar
30 g (1½ oz) self-raising flour
30 g (1½ oz) rolled oats
pinch of salt

Melt butter and sugar. Mix flour, oats and salt and stir into melted butter. Press resulting mix into a greased small swiss roll tin making sure the depth is not over ¼ inch thick. Bake at 350°F, Gas 4, 180°C for about 20 minutes or until nicely browned, and cut into fingers before cooling in the tin.

Biscuits

There is a wide range of biscuit-making methods; some methods are the same as for cakes, in particular the creaming of the butter and sugar. In biscuits, however, this does not have to be quite so meticulously carried out, for it is not lightness we are seeking to achieve. This section has a wide range of flavours and textures, from the very sophisticated and international Florentines and brandy snaps through to custard creams and peanut butter cookies. All have their merits and all are pretty easy to make. If you feel unsure of your abilities in baking, start with biscuits, for they will nearly always work. Shortbreads do need a little careful handling as they require to be well kneaded if they are not to be cracked and tough.

Peanut Butter Cookies

150 g (6 oz) margarine
125 g (5 oz) sugar
125 g (5 oz) soft brown sugar
1 egg
1 ml (¼ teaspoon) vanilla essence
175 g (7 oz) peanut butter (rough)
250 g (10 oz) flour
2.5 ml (½ teaspoon) bicarbonate of soda

Cream fat with both sugars and blend in the egg, vanilla and peanut butter. Sift flour and bicarbonate of soda and fold into the creamed mixture. When thoroughly blended chill for 30 minutes. Form into small balls and roll in granulated sugar and bake on a greased tray for 10–12 minutes at 375°F, Gas 5, 190°C. Cool on a wire rack.

50

Pitcaithly Bannocks

300 g (12 oz) flour
100 g (4 oz) rice flour
200 g (8 oz) butter
100 g (4 oz) caster sugar
50 g (2 oz) chopped almonds
50 g (2 oz) peel
pinch of salt

Sift the flours. In a separate bowl work the butter and sugar together using a wooden spoon. Work in the dry ingredients and knead with the ball of the hand. Keep the dough in a firm lump. Divide in four and roll out to ½ inch thick. Pinch the edges and prick well. Bake in a slow oven (325°F, Gas 3, 160°C) for 30–40 minutes.

Ginger Snaps

100 g (4 oz) butter
100 g (4 oz) sugar
250 g (10 oz) flour
7.5 ml (1½ teaspoons) ground ginger
2.5 ml (½ teaspoon) bicarbonate of soda
45 ml (3 tablespoons) syrup
water

Cream butter and sugar. Add flour and ginger and mix well. Dissolve bicarbonate of soda in a little water and syrup and add to the previous mixture. Form into small balls with floured hands. Bake on greased tins in a hot oven (375°F, Gas 5, 190°C) for 20 minutes. Cool on a wire tray.

Coconut Biscuits

100 g (4 oz) margarine
100 g (4 oz) sugar
225 g (9 oz) flour
5 ml (1 teaspoon) baking powder
1 egg
75 g (3 oz) coconut

Cream margarine and sugar. Sift the flour and baking powder and add to the creamed mixture along with the egg and coconut. Put in teaspoonfuls on a greased baking sheet and bake for approximately 20 minutes at 350°F, Gas 4, 180°C until pale brown. Cool on a wire rack.

Ginger Wafers

100 g (4 oz) butter
150 g (6 oz) sugar
300 g (12 oz) flour
2.5 ml (½ teaspoon) baking powder
25 g (1 oz) ginger
10 ml (2 teaspoons) syrup
60 ml (4 tablespoons) milk

Beat butter and sugar to a cream. Sift in the flour, baking powder and ginger. Heat the syrup and milk and mix into the rest of the ingredients. Roll out thinly and cut in 2-inch rounds. Cook in a moderate oven (350°F, Gas 4, 180°C) for 20–25 minutes. Cool on a wire tray. Makes 36.

Custard Creams

75 g (3 oz) margarine
25 g (1 oz) icing sugar
75 g (3 oz) flour
25 g (1 oz) custard powder

Filling

vanilla-flavoured buttercream

Cream the margarine and sugar well together and add the sifted flour and custard powder. Grease a baking sheet and roll the mixture into small balls. Place them on the sheet and flatten slightly with a fork. Bake at 375°F, Gas 5, 190°C for 15 minutes. Cool on a wire tray and fill with vanilla-flavoured buttercream.

Coconut Thins

150 g (6 oz) butter
100 g (4 oz) plain flour
100 g (4 oz) self raising flour
75 g (3 oz) coconut
50 g (2 oz) caster sugar
2 egg yolks

Rub the butter into the flour and add the coconut and sugar. Add the yolks and mix to a stiff dough. A little milk may be added if required. Knead the mixture lightly. Roll out on a floured board and cut into 2-inch biscuits using a plain cutter. Bake in a moderate oven (350°F, Gas 4, 180°C) for 20–25 minutes. While cooling on a wire tray sprinkle with a little granulated sugar. Makes 24.

Tosca Cookies

150 g (6 oz) butter
75 g (3 oz) ground rice
25 g (1 oz) ground almonds
100 g (4 oz) sugar
100 g (4 oz) flour
1 egg

Topping

50 g (2 oz) butter
75 g (3 oz) sugar
25 ml (¾ tablespoon) maple syrup
25 g (1 oz) flaked almonds

Melt the butter and add the rest of the dry ingredients and the egg. Put in teaspoonfuls on an unbuttered baking sheet. Bake at 350°F, Gas 4, 180°C for 10–12 minutes. Combine butter, sugar and syrup in a small pan. Boil for 2 minutes. Stir in the flaked almonds. Put a little of this mixture on to the top of each biscuit and replace in the oven for a further 5 minutes.

Coffee Kisses

2 egg whites
100 g (4 oz) caster sugar
100 g (4 oz) ground almonds
coffee butter icing

Whisk egg whites until stiff. Mix sugar and almonds and fold into whites. Put in tea-spoonfuls on ungreased baking sheet and bake at 375°F, Gas 5, 190°C for 10–15 minutes or until nicely browned. Cool and sandwich together with coffee butter icing (page 104).

Melting Moments

75 g (3 oz) lard
50 g (2 oz) margarine
75 g (3 oz) sugar
1 egg
150 g (6 oz) flour
crushed cornflakes

Cream fat and sugar until very soft and then beat in the egg and stir in the flour. Form into small balls and roll in crushed cornflakes. Bake in a moderate oven (350°F, Gas 4, 180°C) for 20–25 minutes.

Peppermint Biscuits

225 g (9 oz) margarine
75 g (3 oz) icing sugar
225 g (9 oz) self raising flour
peppermint essence

Cream the margarine and sugar well. Blend the flour in, along with a few drops of peppermint essence. Put in a large forcing bag fitted with a large star pipe (an eight point is the best) and pipe in spirals on to a greased tray. Do not make them too large as they spread in the cooking. Six for an average tray is about right. Bake at 350°F,

Gas 4, 180°C for 20 minutes. Cool on the tray for a little while before moving to a wire rack to cool completely. Use a broad flexible spatula for this as these biscuits are very brittle and break easily.

Peppermint Biscuits

Fife Bannock

150 g (6 oz) flour
pinch of salt
2.5 ml (½ teaspoon) bicarbonate of soda
5 ml (1 teaspoon) cream of tartar
100 g (4 oz) oatmeal
35 g (1½ oz) butter
2.5 ml (½ teaspoon) caster sugar
15 ml (1 tablespoon) buttermilk

Mix the dry ingredients by sifting the flour, salt and raising agents and stirring in the oatmeal. Rub in the butter, add sugar and mix to a scone dough with the milk. Roll out to ½ inch thick in a round. Bake on a fairly hot girdle for 10 minutes.

Orange Jumbles

75 g (3 oz) butter
100 g (4 oz) caster sugar
rind and juice of 2 lemons
50 g (2 oz) flour
100 g (4 oz) finely chopped almonds
drop of cochineal

Cream the butter and sugar and beat in the juice, rind and flour. Add the almonds and colouring. Drop in teaspoonfuls wide apart on a greased baking sheet, as they spread in cooking. Bake in a moderate oven (350°F, Gas 4, 180°C) for about 15 minutes. Cool on the sheet for a moment before transferring to a wire tray.

Rich Scotch Shortbread

½ kilo (1 lb) flour
100 g (4 oz) caster sugar
200 g (8 oz) butter

Sift the flour, add the sugar and cut in the butter in pieces the size of a walnut. Rub in the butter and knead to a solid thick lump. When you have all the flour incorporated and the dough smooth, roll out thickly and prick all over with a fork. Cut into fingers and lay these on a dry baking sheet. Bake in a hot oven (425°F, Gas 7, 220°C) for 10 minutes and then lower the heat to 350°F, Gas 4, 180°C for about an hour until a nice golden brown colour. Cool a little before removing to a wire tray.

Shortbread

350 g (14 oz) flour
50 g (2 oz) rice flour
100 g (4 oz) caster sugar
225 g (9 oz) butter, cut into chunks

Sift the flours into a bowl, and in the middle put the sugar and the butter. Knead butter and the sugar together at first and gradually work in the flours. Knead until quite smooth. Divide in two and shape the pieces in two rounds about $\frac{1}{4}$ inch thick. Prick the middles and decorate the edges by pinching them all round, in the traditional manner. A shortbread mould may be used if preferred. Bake in a moderate oven (350°F, Gas 4, 180°C) for about 40–45 minutes or until a nice brown all over. Cool. Sprinkle with caster sugar.

Macaroons (1)

10 ml (1 tablespoon) ground rice
200 g (8 oz) caster sugar
100 g (4 oz) ground almonds
drop of vanilla essence
3 egg whites

Combine the ground rice with the sugar and ground almonds. Whip the egg whites until stiff and fold in the dry ingredients with a drop of vanilla essence. Drop in teaspoonfuls on to a sheet of rice paper on a baking sheet. Bake at 375°F, Gas 5, 190°C for about 20 minutes or until browned.

Macaroons (2)

2 egg whites
200 g (8 oz) icing sugar
100 g (4 oz) ground almonds
whole almonds

Whip the egg whites until stiff and fold in the sugar and ground almonds. Put in rough heaps on non-stick paper and press an almond in the middle of each. Bake at 375°F, Gas 5, 190°C for about 20 minutes or until nicely browned. Cool on a wire rack.

Gypsy Creams

75 g (3 oz) flour
50 g (2 oz) margarine
50 g (2 oz) lard
75 g (3 oz) sugar
5 ml (1 teaspoon) syrup
15 ml (1 tablespoon) boiling water
2.5 ml ($\frac{1}{2}$ teaspoon) bicarbonate of soda
100 g (4 oz) rolled oats
25 g (1 oz) cocoa

Filling

50 g (2 oz) butter
15 ml (1 tablespoon) syrup
30 ml (2 tablespoons) cocoa

For the biscuits, cream the fats and sugar. Add syrup and water and beat in. Mix the dry ingredients and add them to the

54

creamed mix. When well blended, roll into small balls and place on a greased baking sheet. Bake for 20 minutes at 350°F, Gas 4, 180°C. Cool on a wire rack. For the filling, cream the butter and syrup and add the cocoa. Beat well. Cover half the biscuits with this and top with the rest. *Illustrated in colour opposite page 56.*

Abernethy Biscuits

50 g (2 oz) sugar
30 ml (2 tablespoons) milk
250 g (10 oz) flour
5 ml (1 teaspoon) cream of tartar
5 ml (1 teaspoon) bicarbonate of soda
pinch of salt
75 g (3 oz) margarine
50 g (2 oz) lard

Melt the sugar in the milk and cool. Sift the dry ingredients and rub in the fats. Add the sugar and milk and bind to a stiff dough. Roll out to a ¼ inch thick and cut in 2- to 2½-inch rounds. Prick well and bake at 375°F, Gas 5, 190°C for about 15 minutes. Cool on a rack.

Almond Shortbread

100 g (4 oz) butter
200 g (8 oz) flour
100 g (4 oz) caster sugar
1 egg
drop of vanilla essence
50 g (2 oz) chopped almonds
25 g (1 oz) demerara sugar

Work the butter into the flour and the caster sugar using the heat of the hand to mix. Add the egg and vanilla and lastly most of the finely chopped almonds. Bind and knead well. Form into a long roll about 2 inches in diameter. Roll in the rest of the almonds and demerara sugar mixed. Chill. Cut in thick slices and lay on a baking sheet. Bake for 30 minutes at 350°F, Gas 4, 180°C, or until nicely browned.

Almond Shortbread

55

Brandy Shortbread

100 g (4 oz) butter
150 g (6 oz) flour
50 g (2 oz) sugar
15 ml (1 tablespoon) brandy
white of an egg, beaten
nibbed almonds

Rub the butter into the flour and add the sugar. Add the brandy and mix to a stiff dough. Roll out to ¼ inch thick and cut into fingers. Brush the top with a little beaten egg white and sprinkle with a few nibbed almonds. Bake at 350°F, Gas 4, 180°C for 15–20 minutes.

Afghans

175 g (7 oz) butter
50 g (2 oz) sugar
10 ml (2 teaspoons) cocoa
150 g (6 oz) flour
5 ml (1 teaspoon) baking powder
50 g (2 oz) crushed cornflakes
5 ml (1 teaspoon) vanilla essence
chocolate water icing (page 104)
walnuts

Cream the fat and the sugar and add the sifted dry ingredients. Stir in and then add the cornflakes. Beat into the mix, with the vanilla. Take small pieces and make into rough heaps on a greased baking sheet. Bake at 350°F, Gas 4, 180°C for 20 minutes. Cool on a wire tray and top with a little chocolate icing and a half walnut.

56

Brandy Snaps

50 g (2 oz) sugar
50 g (2 oz) butter
50 g (2 oz) flour
30 ml (2 tablespoons) syrup
5 ml (1 teaspoon) ground ginger

Put all the ingredients into a small pan and warm them together gently. Drop in teaspoonfuls on to a greased tray leaving three inches between for them to spread. Bake for 7–10 minutes at 350°F, Gas 4, 180°C. Grease the handles of as many wooden spoons as you have and after cooling for a few seconds roll quickly round the handles. When they start to set slip off on to a wire tray. Fill with whipped cream.

Australian Biscuits

200 g (8 oz) butter
100 g (4 oz) soft brown sugar
2 egg yolks
30 ml (2 tablespoons) single cream
10 ml (2 teaspoons) vinegar
10 ml (2 teaspoons) bicarbonate of soda
½ kilo (1 lb) flour
5 ml (1 teaspoon) nutmeg
5 ml (1 teaspoon) cinnamon
pinch of salt
100 g (4 oz) raisins

Cream the butter and sugar. Add the yolks of the eggs and beat in. Mix the cream, vinegar, and baking soda and beat into the butter mixture. Add the flour and the rest

Chocolate Kisses (left) and Gypsy Creams

Coconut Cupids (left) and Florentines

Almond Cheesecakes (left) and Jap Cakes

of the dry ingredients. Stir in the raisins, and chill for several hours. Roll out to an eighth of an inch thick and cut into 2-inch rounds. Put on an ungreased tray and bake for 10 minutes at 350°F, Gas 4, 180°C. While still warm sprinkle with a little sugar. Makes about 50.

Shortbread Biscuits

150 g (6 oz) margarine
50 g (2 oz) caster sugar
200 g (8 oz) flour
10 ml (2 teaspoons) ground rice

Cream the margarine and sugar and add the flour and ground rice. Blend well and knead lightly. Roll out to about ¼ inch thick and cut in rounds with a fluted cutter. Prick with a fork. Bake on a greased baking sheet for 20 minutes at 350°F, Gas 4, 180°C.

Cherry Biscuits

75 g (3 oz) margarine
75 g (3 oz) sugar
1 egg
5 ml (1 teaspoon) vanilla essence
glacé cherries
150 g (6 oz) self raising flour
pinch of salt

Cream the margarine and sugar. Beat in the egg and the essence. Chop the cherries

finely and add with the flour and the salt to the creamed mixture. Form into little balls and place on a greased baking sheet. Bake for 15–20 minutes at 375°F, Gas 5, 190°C.

Chocolate Kisses

2 egg whites
50 g (2 oz) chocolate powder
300 g (12 oz) caster sugar
vanilla essence

Whip the egg whites until stiff. Mix the chocolate powder with the sugar and fold into the egg whites. Add a few drops of vanilla. Drop in rough heaps (about a tablespoon will do) onto rice paper. Bake in a moderate oven (350°F, Gas 4, 180°C) for 15 minutes. These may be served as they are, or with vanilla-flavoured cream in the middle of two. *Illustrated in colour opposite page 56.*

Tantallon Biscuits

Base

100 g (4 oz) butter
200 g (8 oz) flour
50 g (2 oz) sugar
2 egg yolks

Top

150–200 g (6–8 oz) icing sugar
2 egg whites
2.5 ml (½ teaspoon) cream of tartar
chopped nibbed almonds

For the base, rub the butter into the flour and add the sugar. Use the yolks to form a stiff paste and knead well until the mixture is smooth. Roll out to a $\frac{1}{4}$-inch thick and cut into strips $2\frac{1}{2}$ to 3 inches wide. Place on a baking sheet.

To make the topping, add the icing sugar to the lightly beaten egg whites with the cream of tartar. When a spreading consistency is achieved spread on the strips. Decorate the edges of the strips with chopped nibbed almonds and leave for 15 minutes to set. Mark in fingers and bake at 325°F, Gas 3, 160°C for 10–15 minutes. Separate into fingers to cool.

Ginger Creams

100 g (4 oz) margarine
100 g (4 oz) sugar
1 egg
10 ml (2 teaspoons) syrup
100 g (4 oz) flour
7.5 ml (1½ teaspoons) baking powder
75 g (3 oz) cornflour
2.5 ml (½ teaspoon) ginger

Filling

25 g (1 oz) butter or margarine
50 g (2 oz) icing sugar
5 ml (1 teaspoon) ginger syrup

Cream the fat and sugar and add the egg. Beat in well with the syrup. Sift the dry ingredients and stir in. Put in small teaspoonfuls on a greased baking sheet. Cook at 375°F, Gas 5, 190°C for about 15 minutes. Cool and then fill with a ginger flavoured icing, made by creaming the butter or margarine and beating in the icing sugar and ginger syrup.

Ginger Biscuits

½ kilo (1 lb) flour
20 g (¾ oz) ginger
200 g (8 oz) soft brown sugar
200 g (8 oz) butter
300 g (12 oz) treacle

Mix the flour and the ginger by sifting into a bowl. Melt the sugar, butter and treacle and pour into the dry ingredients. Blend thoroughly and stand to cool. When cold roll out on a lightly floured board and cut into biscuits using a 1½ inch cutter. Bake on a greased tray at 350°F, Gas 4, 180°C for 15 minutes.

Florentines (1)

75 g (3 oz) butter
100 g (4 oz) caster sugar
100 g (4 oz) mixed nuts
25 g (1 oz) glacé cherries
25 g (1 oz) mixed peel
15 g (¾ oz) flour
100 g (4 oz) chocolate

Melt the butter and add the sugar. Dissolve it gradually over a low heat and then allow to boil slowly for a minute. Add the chopped nuts, chopped cherries and the mixed peel. Stir in the flour and allow the mix to cool a little, but not too much or it will become hard. Put in well-spaced-out heaps on non-stick paper on baking sheets. Bake at 350°F, Gas 4, 180°C for 10 minutes or until golden. Take them out and at this stage you can tidy up the edges with a spatula. Cool on paper at first and then on a wire tray. When cold melt the chocolate and spread on the base of the biscuits. As the chocolate starts to set draw wavy lines on it with the tines of a fork. *Illustrated in colour between pages 56 and 57.*

Florentines (2)

100 g (4 oz) caster sugar
50 g (2 oz) butter
100 ml (4 fl oz) double cream
150 g (6 oz) nibbed almonds
40 g (1½ oz) plain flour
40 g (1½ oz) mixed peel
chocolate

Put the sugar, butter and cream in a small pan and heat. Bring to the boil. Mix the almonds, flour and peel together and stir into the butter mix. When thoroughly blended put in teaspoonfuls on non-stick paper on a baking sheet 3 inches apart. Bake at 350°F, Gas 4, 180°C for 15 minutes. Tidy the edges if they have spread too far. Cool for a few minutes on the paper and then transfer to a wire rack. Melt the chocolate and when the biscuits are cold spread the back of each with a thin layer. When half-set draw wavy lines with a fork on the chocolate.

Caramel Wafer Biscuits

150 g (6 oz) butter or margarine
250 g (10 oz) brown sugar
400 g (1 lb) flour
5 ml (1 teaspoon) bicarbonate of soda
5 ml (1 teaspoon) cream of tartar
pinch of salt
2 eggs

Cream the butter and sugar and add the flour sifted with the bicarbonate of soda and cream of tartar and salt. Bind with the eggs lightly beaten. Form the mixture into a roll of about 2 inches diameter and slice thinly. Put on a baking sheet and bake at 375°F, Gas 5, 190°C for 10–15 minutes.

Cheese Straws

50 g (2 oz) butter
50 g (2 oz) flour
75 g (3 oz) cheese, finely grated
cayenne pepper
salt
egg yolk and water

Rub the butter into the flour and add the cheese. Mix in seasonings. Bind the mixture with a little egg yolk and water mixed. Roll out on a well-floured board and cut with a sharp knife into fingers or rings. Put on a floured baking sheet and bake at 400°F, Gas 6, 200°C for about 10 minutes or until lightly browned. Nicest served hot.

Coconut Cupids

50 g (2 oz) margarine
50 g (2 oz) sugar
10 ml (2 teaspoons) beaten egg
50 g (2 oz) flour
65 g (2½ oz) coconut
glacé cherries

Cream the fat and sugar and beat in the egg and flour. Fold in the coconut. Make into small balls and place on a buttered tray. Flatten slightly with a fork and put a small bit of cherry in the middle. Bake at 350°F, Gas 4, 180°C for 15 minutes. *Illustrated in colour between pages 56 and 57.*

Easter Biscuits

100 g (4 oz) margarine
100 g (4 oz) sugar
1 egg
few drops vanilla essence
220 g (8 oz) flour
75 g (3 oz) currants

Cream the margarine and sugar together and add the egg and beat it in. Stir in the essence and add the flour and finally the currants. Mix thoroughly and roll out on a floured baking board. Cut in rounds and place on a baking sheet. Bake for 10 minutes at 375°F, Gas 5, 190°C. Makes about 12.

Cinnamon Biscuits

75 g (3 oz) butter
75 g (3 oz) sugar
150 g (6 oz) flour
5 ml (1 teaspoon) cinnamon
1 egg
25 g (1 oz) nibbed almonds

Beat the butter and sugar to a cream. Mix the flour and cinnamon and stir in with the egg forming a stiff dough. Roll out on a floured board and cut into rounds with a fluted cutter. Sprinkle with a few almonds and bake in a moderate oven (350°F, Gas 4, 180°C) for about 15 minutes. Cool on a wire rack.

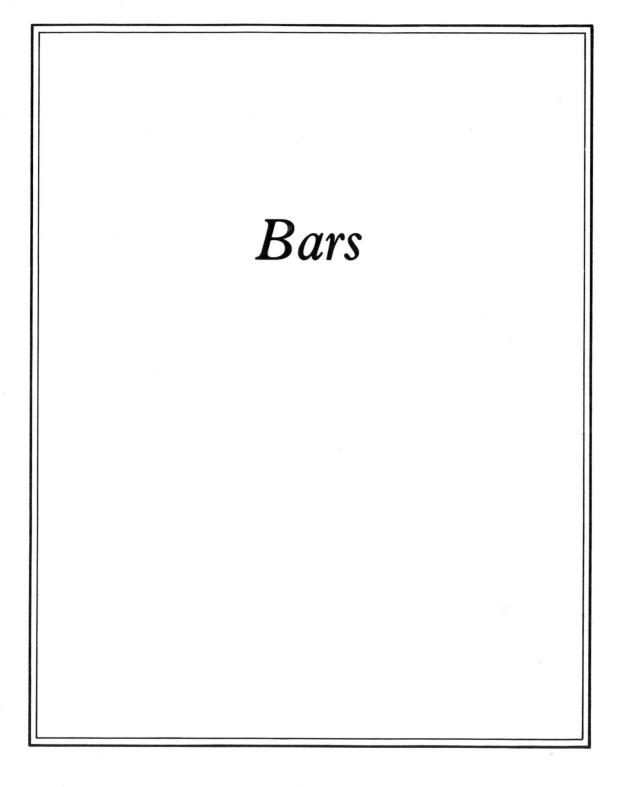

Bars

Bars, tray bakes, slices, squares, call them what you will, this chapter is about the goodies cooked in shallow trays and cut up into pieces to suit your needs, and also to suit the richness of the contents. Some are cut as large as two inches square and others can only be cut into small fingers, for they are quite rich. Most of the tray bakes I have included are done in a standard swiss roll tin, except where a small swiss roll tin is specified. Some, such as the fruit squares, require a tin at least 1- to 1½-inches deep. Incidentally, this fruit square is not the usual 'squashed fly' one, but a much lighter confection, which is equally delicious served warm with cream for a pudding or cold for tea. The majority of recipes in this section are biscuit-type, but there are some cakes, such as chocolate gingerbread and picnic cake, which are excellent, as is the maple syrup gingercake.

Date and Walnut Slice

2 eggs
200 g (8 oz) caster sugar
25 g (1 oz) flour
2.5 ml (½ teaspoon) baking powder
pinch of salt
200 g (8 oz) dates
200 g (8 oz) walnuts

Beat eggs and sugar until light and fluffy. Add the flour sifted with baking powder and salt. Add chopped fruit and nuts and spread this mixture in a well-greased swiss roll tin. Bake for 25 minutes at 350°F, Gas 4, 180°C. Cool in the tray and then cut in slices. Makes about 24.

Chocolate Crunch

200 g (8 oz) digestive biscuits
100 g (4 oz) icing sugar
250 g (10 oz) chocolate
200 g (8 oz) margarine
2.5 ml (½ teaspoon) vanilla essence
100 g (4 oz) currants

Crush the digestive biscuits, but not too finely. Add icing sugar. Put chocolate in a bowl with the margarine and melt over a pan of hot water. When melted add the vanilla. Stir in the currants and biscuit mix. Butter a swiss roll tin and pour in the mixture. Smooth over with a spatula and allow to set. Cut into 24 pieces.

Picnic Cake with Icing

Cake

300 g (12 oz) sugar
200 g (8 oz) flour
100 g (4 oz) butter or margarine
100 g (4 oz) white cooking fat
45 ml (3 tablespoons) cocoa
1 cup water
½ cup milk
5 ml (1 teaspoon) bicarbonate of soda
2 eggs
1 teaspoon vanilla essence

Icing

100 g (4 oz) margarine
50 g (2 oz) chocolate

60 ml (4 tablespoons) strong coffee
½ kilo (1 lb) icing sugar
50 g (2 oz) chopped walnuts
5 ml (1 teaspoon) vanilla essence

Mix sugar and flour. Melt butter or margarine, white fat, cocoa and water in a pan and bring to the boil. Mix in the flour and sugar and add milk, soda, eggs and lastly the vanilla. Beat well. Pour into a greased and floured swiss roll tin. Bake for 15 to 20 minutes at 400°F, Gas 6, 200°C. Cool.

Make the icing by melting the margarine and chocolate with the coffee. Pour on to the sifted icing sugar and beat well. Add the chopped nuts and the vanilla and spread over the picnic cake. When cooled and set cut into squares. Keeps well.

Date Fingers

200 g (8 oz) flour
10 ml (2 teaspoons) baking powder
pinch of salt
150 g (6 oz) caster sugar
2 eggs
15 ml (1 tablespoon) butter
75 g (3 oz) chopped walnuts
½ kilo (1 lb) dates
15 ml (1 tablespoon) hot water

Sift dry ingredients. Beat sugar and eggs together until light, and then add the butter and beat again. Beat in the nuts and finely chopped dates. Stir in dry ingredients and hot water. Beat well, and then spread in a greased and floured swiss

roll tin. Bake at 350°F, Gas 4, 180°C for 25 minutes. Cool slightly and then cut into 1-inch wide fingers. While still warm, roll lightly in granulated sugar.

Crunchy Coconut Squares

1 cup self raising flour
1 cup cornflakes
1 cup coconut
½ cup sugar
100 g (4 oz) margarine

Mix the dry ingredients. Melt the margarine and pour into the dry ingredients. Mix well. Press into a small swiss roll tin and bake at 350°F, Gas 4, 180°C for 25 minutes. Cut while hot into squares and allow to cool. In the middle of each put a spoonful of plain glacé icing.

Crunchy Slice

200 g (8 oz) plain chocolate
50 g (2 oz) margarine
100 g (4 oz) soft brown sugar
1 egg
25 g (1 oz) coconut
25 g (1 oz) glacé cherries
25 g (1 oz) mixed peel
25 g (1 oz) sultanas
50 g (2 oz) Jordans Crunchy

Butter a swiss roll tin and in it melt the chocolate. Set. Cream the margarine and sugar and add the egg. Beat well. Add the coconut, the fruit and the Crunchy and stir in thoroughly. Bake for 30 minutes at 325°F, Gas 3, 160°C until set. Cool. Cut into 24 squares.

Caramel Lunch Squares

100 g (4 oz) margarine
150 g (6 oz) sugar
2 eggs, separated
200 g (8 oz) flour
10 ml (2 teaspoons) baking powder
100 g (4 oz) soft brown sugar
75 g (3 oz) walnuts

Cream margarine and sugar and add the yolks. Sift in flour and baking powder. Press into a greased swiss roll tin. Beat the whites until stiff, and add the brown sugar and nuts. Put on top of the pastry base. Cook in a moderate oven (350°F, Gas 4, 180°C) for 20 minutes. Cool for a while before marking into squares.

Chocolate Nut Bars

100 g (4 oz) margarine
100 g (4 oz) sugar
1 egg
150 g (6 oz) flour
5 ml (1 teaspoon) cocoa
5 ml (1 teaspoon) baking powder
vanilla
50 g (2 oz) cornflakes
75 g (3 oz) walnuts, chopped
75 g (3 oz) coconut

Cream margarine and sugar. Add the egg and beat hard. Mix in the flour, cocoa, baking powder and vanilla. Add cornflakes, chopped nuts and coconut. Mix well and press into a greased swiss roll tin. Bake for 30 minutes at 350°F, Gas 4, 180°C. Ice with chocolate water icing (page 104) and cut into bars.

Brownies

50 g (2 oz) plain chocolate
75 g (3 oz) margarine
2 eggs
75 g (3 oz) sugar
100 g (4 oz) self raising flour
2.5 ml (½ teaspoon) salt
25 g (1 oz) chopped nuts

Melt chocolate and margarine over hot water. Beat in the eggs and sugar. Mix in the flour and salt and fold in the nuts. Cook in a greased 8-inch square tin for 30 to 35 minutes at 350°F, Gas 4, 180°C. Cool slightly and cut into squares.

Cheese Cake with Sour Cream Topping

Base

50 g (2 oz) butter
200 g (8 oz) digestive biscuit crumbs
1 tablespoon sugar

Filling

½ kilo (1 lb) cream cheese
5 eggs
150 g (6 oz) sugar
5 ml (1 teaspoon) vanilla essence

Topping

12 fl oz sour cream
50 g (2 oz) caster sugar
5 ml (1 teaspoon) vanilla essence

For the base melt the butter and mix in the biscuit crumbs and sugar. Line a 10-inch by 10-inch square tin with non-stick paper and press the mixture into the base in an even layer. Soften the cream cheese by beating it well and beat in the eggs, sugar and vanilla. When it is quite smooth pour over the base carefully. Set in the oven (300°F, Gas 2, 150°C) for 1 hour. Combine the sour cream with the sugar and vanilla and pour on top. Stand for 5 minutes. Raise the oven temperature to 350°F, Gas 4, 180°C and bake for a further 10 minutes. If this topping still appears a bit

runny in the middle do not worry. It will set once the cake is cool. Chill thoroughly when cold and cut into squares for serving.

Paradise Cake

150 g (6 oz) melt-in-the-mouth pastry
  (page 25)
raspberry jam
100 g (4 oz) margarine
100 g (4 oz) sugar
1 egg
30 ml (2 tablespoons) ground rice
50 g (2 oz) glacé cherries
50 g (2 oz) walnuts
30 ml (2 tablespoons) ground almonds
100 g (4 oz) sultanas

Line a swiss roll tin with the pastry and spread on a layer of jam. Cream margarine and sugar and add the egg. Beat well. Stir in the rest of the ingredients. Spread this mix over the jam and bake at 350°F, Gas 4, 180°C for 30 to 35 minutes. Cut into fingers.

Paradise Cake

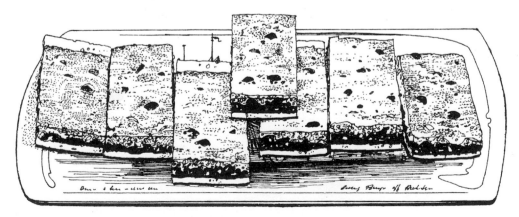

Cocoa Crispy Bars

100 g (4 oz) toffee bars
50 g (2 oz) margarine
100 g (4 oz) marshmallows
60 to 70 g (2 to 3 oz) rice crispies
15 ml (1 tablespoon) cocoa

Butter a small deep tin. Melt margarine and toffee bars in a pan over a very low heat to prevent burning. When the toffee is mostly melted add the marshmallows and stir. Leave until completely melted. Mix in the rice crispies with the cocoa until most of the toffee mix is absorbed. Lightly press mix into the tin and allow to cool. Cut into bars. Makes about 12.

Coconut Squares

125 g (5 oz) butter
1 cup self raising flour
1 cup cornflakes
1 cup rolled oats
1 cup coconut
75 g (3 oz) sugar

Melt butter and stir in all the rest of the ingredients. Butter a swiss roll tin and press the mixture into it. Bake for 20 to 25 minutes in a moderately hot oven (375°F, Gas 5, 190°C). Drizzle plain white glacé icing over the top in a random pattern. When the icing is set, cut in squares. Makes 24.

Coconut Squares

Maple Syrup Gingercake

225 g (9 oz) flour
10 ml (2 teaspoons) ginger
5 ml (1 teaspoon) bicarbonate of soda
pinch of salt
50 g (2 oz) butter
1 cup (6 fl oz) maple syrup
1 cup (6 fl oz) sour cream
1 egg

Sift the dry ingredients. Melt the butter and mix the maple syrup with the sour cream and the egg. Add the butter and then beat in the dry ingredients. Beat well. Bake in an 8-inch by 12-inch lined tin at 350°F, Gas 4, 180°C for 30 minutes. Cool and cut in squares.

Fruit Fingers

150 g (6 oz) short pastry
red jam
1 egg
50 g (2 oz) ground almonds
100 g (4 oz) caster sugar
50 g (2 oz) chopped glacé cherries
50 g (2 oz) raisins

Line a swiss roll tin with the pastry and spread liberally with jam. Beat the egg to a stiff froth and add the dry ingredients and fruits. Spread on the top of the jam and cook in a moderately hot oven (375°F, Gas 5, 190°C) until the pastry is cooked and the top is nicely brown. This should take about 15 minutes. Cut into fingers.

Fudge Fingers

100 g (4 oz) margarine
150 g (6 oz) self raising flour
salt
150 g (6 oz) sugar
50 g (2 oz) glacé cherries
50 g (2 oz) walnuts
30 ml (1 tablespoon) coconut
10 ml (2 teaspoons) cocoa
1 egg
icing sugar

Rub the fat into the flour and salt and add the sugar, chopped fruit and nuts, coconut and cocoa. Beat the egg lightly in a small bowl and add the mixture. Press into a small swiss roll tin that has been well buttered and bake for 20 minutes at 375°F, Gas 5, 190°C. Cut in strips while still hot. When quite cold dust with icing sugar.

Ginger Biscuits

200 g (8 oz) butter or margarine
300 g (12 oz) sugar
3 eggs
30 ml (2 tablespoons) milk
30 ml (2 tablespoons) ginger
300 g (12 oz) flour to stiffen

Cream the butter and sugar and beat in the eggs and milk. Add the ginger and enough of the flour to form a stiff dough. Spread on a greased swiss roll tin and mark in fingers. Bake at 350°F, Gas 4, 180°C for about 20 to 25 minutes.

Chocolate Coconut Fingers

200 g (8 oz) chocolate
1 egg
100 g (4 oz) caster sugar
100 g (4 oz) coconut
50 g (2 oz) sultanas
50 g (2 oz) glacé cherries

Line the bottom of a swiss roll tin with melted chocolate. Beat the egg and add to the sugar, coconut and fruits. Mix well and spread on top of hardened chocolate. Bake for 15 to 20 minutes at 350°F, Gas 4, 180°C until golden. Leave in tin until cold. Cut into fingers and turn out.

Millionaire Shortbread

Base

150 g (6 oz) margarine
75 g (3 oz) caster sugar
125 g (9 oz) flour

Filling

150 g (6 oz) margarine
100 g (4 oz) sugar
1 large tin condensed milk
60 ml (4 tablespoons) syrup

Topping

150 g (6 oz) chocolate
25 g (1 oz) butter

For the base, cream the margarine and sugar and add the flour. This is a very sticky pastry. Spread evenly into a greased swiss roll tin. Bake for 20 minutes at 350°F, Gas 4, 180°C until golden brown. Cool. For the filling, melt the margarine, sugar and the milk with the syrup in a heavy-based pan, preferably a copper sweet-pan. When the sugar is all dissolved, bring to the boil and allow to boil undisturbed for five minutes. Take off the heat and beat well for three minutes. An electric hand mixer is the best for this as it produces a fudge-like consistency. After three minutes pour over the pastry base and allow to cool. Melt the chocolate for the topping with the butter and mix together. Pour over the toffee and spread evenly over the surface. Cool. When set cut into 24 squares. The way these disappear you might as well start again at once!

Honey Fruit Slice

30 ml (2 tablespoons) potato flour
30 ml (2 tablespoons) water
200 g (8 oz) honey
25 g (1 oz) butter
60 ml (4 tablespoons) lemon juice
150 g (6 oz) currants
150 g (6 oz) raisins or sultanas
50 g (2 oz) preserved orange peel
200 g (½ lb) rough puff pastry (page 25)

Mix the potato flour to a paste with cold water. Add to the honey, butter and lemon juice. Add the fruits and put on a low heat to thicken the filling. Stir all the time allowing about 2 to 3 minutes. Cool. Roll the pastry to approximately 10 inches by

4 inches and damp the edges. Put the filling in the middle and fold the pastry over like a large sausage roll. Seal. Brush the top with egg and sprinkle with sugar. Slash the pastry at intervals and place on a damp baking sheet. Bake for 30 minutes in a hot oven (425°F, Gas 7, 220°C). Use either hot or cold cut in half-inch thick pieces.

Chocolate Peppermint Bars

Base

100 g (4 oz) margarine
50 g (2 oz) sugar
150 g (6 oz) flour
50 g (2 oz) cocoa

Filling

75 g (3 oz) margarine
125 g (5 oz) icing sugar
peppermint essence
green colouring

Topping

150 g (6 oz) plain chocolate
25 g (1 oz) butter

Make the base by creaming the margarine and sugar and then add the sifted flour and cocoa. Work to a stiff paste and press into a greased swiss roll tin. Bake at 350°F, Gas 4, 180°C for 20 to 25 minutes until set. Cool. Cream the margarine and sugar for the filling and add peppermint essence to taste.

Add a very few drops of green colouring and beat in. The colouring is very strong so do take care not to add too much. Spread over the cold base. Melt the chocolate and butter in a basin over hot water and spread carefully over the peppermint filling. Leave to set. Cut into 24 squares.

Peppermint Sticks

150 g (6 oz) margarine
150 g (6 oz) flour
100 g (4 oz) coconut
100 g (4 oz) sugar
40 ml (3 dessertspoons) cocoa
5 ml (1 teaspoon) baking powder
2.5 ml (½ teaspoon) peppermint essence
1 cupful cornflakes

Icing

75 g (3 oz) margarine
100 g (4 oz) icing sugar
peppermint essence
25 g (1 oz) chocolate
15 ml (1 tablespoon) margarine

Melt margarine in a small pan and add the flour, coconut, sugar, cocoa and baking powder. Lastly stir in the essence and cornflakes lightly crushed. Mix well. Grease a swiss roll tin and press the mixture into the tin, making it about a quarter of an inch thick. Bake in a moderate oven (350°F, Gas 4, 180°C) for 20 minutes. Cool in the tray. Cream the margarine and icing sugar and flavour to taste with the peppermint essence. Spread over the biscuit base and roughen with the edge of the knife. Melt the chocolate and beat in the margarine. Drizzle this randomly over the top. Allow to set. Cut into fingers for serving. Makes about 24.

Almond Orange Shortbread

200 g (8 oz) margarine
100 g (4 oz) sugar
5 ml (1 teaspoon) vanilla essence
rind of an orange
150 g (6 oz) flour
100 g (4 oz) almond paste

Cream the margarine and sugar. Add the vanilla and finely grated rind of the orange. Work in the flour. Ease half of this pastry into an 8-inch by 8-inch greased tin. Have the marzipan firm and grate it, using a coarse grater, over the surface. Roll out the rest of the pastry to fit the top and put it in place. Mark in squares before putting in the oven at 325°F, Gas 3, 160°C for an hour. The edges should be a light fawn colour. Re-mark the squares and leave to cool in the tin. These are very rich and it is advisable to make the squares quite small.

Date Bars

200 g (8 oz) dates
125 ml (5 fl oz) water
5 ml (1 teaspoon) vanilla essence
100 g (4 oz) self raising flour
100 g (4 oz) rolled oats
100 g (4 oz) margarine

150 g (6 oz) caster sugar
5 ml (1 teaspoon) bicarbonate of soda

Grease and line an 8-inch square tin approximately 2 inches deep. Chop dates and put in the water and bring to the boil. Simmer until the fruit is soft. Add vanilla. Mix dry ingredients together and rub in the fat. Put a layer of this mix in the base of the lined tin and carefully spread in the date mix. The easiest way to do this is to put spoonfuls all over the top as close as possible and allow it to spread during the baking process. Top with the rest of the mixture; bake in oven at 350°F, Gas 4, 180°C for 20 to 30 minutes until golden brown. Mark in fingers while still hot and cool in the tin. Makes about 18 fingers.

Chocolate Gingerbread

150 ml (6 fl oz) syrup
5 ml (1 teaspoon) ginger
2.5 ml (½ teaspoon) each of mace and
  salt
5 ml (1 teaspoon) bicarbonate of soda
300 g (12 oz) flour
60 ml (4 tablespoons) chocolate powder
75 g (3 oz) sultanas
75 ml (3 fl oz) sour milk

Mix the syrup with the ginger, mace and salt. Stir the bicarbonate of soda in a little water. Add to the warmed syrup and stir in the flour, chocolate, sultanas and sour milk. Make into a dough and put into a greased, shallow, 10-inch square tin. Bake in a moderate oven (350°F, Gas 4, 180°C) for about 20 to 30 minutes.

Small Cakes

In this section I have placed such diverse recipes as jap cakes, which are delicious airy macaroons filled with light butter cream, whipped cream walnuts which require no cooking, and orange rock cakes, which while they sound hard are delicious when eaten fresh and slightly warm. Apricot cakes are nice and a little unusual in that they rely for flavour on the inclusion of apricot jam. The same rules apply for making small cakes as large cakes; proper creaming and light handling, are the secrets of success.

Almond Cheesecakes

200 g (8 oz) melt-in-the-mouth pastry
   (page 26)
50 g (2 oz) margarine
50 g (2 oz) sugar
1 egg
almond essence
15 ml (1 tablespoon) ground rice
ground almonds
grated rind of a lemon
little milk

Use the pastry to line 18 to 24 little patty tins. Cream the margarine and sugar until very light. Beat in the egg and a few drops almond essence. Fold in the ground rice and the almonds and lemon rind. Add enough milk to form a thick batter. Put a little of the mixture in each patty tin. Bake at 350°F, Gas 4, 180°C for 10 to 15 minutes. *Illustrated in colour opposite page 57.*

72

Viennese Whirls

200 g (8 oz) margarine
75 g (3 oz) icing sugar
vanilla essence
200 g (8 oz) flour

Beat the margarine until it becomes very soft. Add the sugar and vanilla essence to taste. Beat until very light and fluffy. Add flour and work it in. Put in a large forcing bag with a star pipe. Pipe into paper cases in a spiral, leaving a small hollow in the middle. Cook for 20 minutes at 350°F, Gas 4, 180°C. Cool. Dust with icing sugar and in the middle put a drop of red jam or lemon curd. Melted chocolate is another alternative.

Rock Cakes

½ kilo (1 lb) self raising flour
100 g (4 oz) sugar
25 g (1 oz) chopped peel
100 g (4 oz) currants
150 g (6 oz) butter
2 eggs
little milk

Mix all the dry ingredients including the fruit. Rub the butter into the dry ingredients. Beat the eggs with about a tablespoon of milk and stir into the dry mixture. Stir in well and put in rough heaps on a greased baking sheet. Bake for 20 minutes at 400°F, Gas 6, 200°C.

Cornflour Shorties

100 g (4 oz) cornflour
75 g (3 oz) flour
125 g (5 oz) butter
75 g (3 oz) caster sugar
almond essence
few whole almonds

Sift the flour and the cornflour until well mixed. Cream the butter and beat in the sugar and the almond essence. Add the flours to the butter mix and drop in spoonfuls into greased patty tins. Place a whole almond on the top of each one and bake for about 20 minutes at 375°F, Gas 5, 190°C.

Orange Rock Cakes

200 g (8 oz) flour
75 g (3 oz) caster sugar
10 ml (2 teaspoons) baking powder
75 ml (3 oz) butter
1 egg
rind and juice of 1 orange

Mix the dry ingredients. Rub in the butter and add the grated rind of the orange. Mix to a stiff dough with the orange juice and the egg. With a fork drop in rough heaps on a greased baking sheet. Cook at 375°F, Gas 5, 190°C for 10 to 15 minutes. Makes 12.

Orange Rock Cakes

Jap Cakes

4 egg whites
225 g (9 oz) caster sugar
125 g (5 oz) ground almonds
coffee butter icing (page 104)

Beat the egg whites until firm. Add a little of the sugar and beat again until stiff. Fold in the rest of the sugar and the almonds. Pipe on to greased baking sheets in even sized rounds of about $1\frac{1}{2}$ inches. Bake at 350°F, Gas 4, 180°C for 25 minutes. Cool on a wire tray. Bake three or four of the cakes quite hard and crush them into coarse crumbs. Sandwich the rounds with the butter icing and carefully cover the edges. Roll in the crumbs to coat the sides completely. Pipe the tops with a circle of tiny buttercream stars all round the edges and in the middle of each place a drop of pink icing or melted chocolate. *Illustrated in colour opposite page 57.*

Ground Rice Cheesecakes

100 g (4 oz) pastry (page 24)
50 g (2 oz) butter
50 g (2 oz) sugar
1 egg
15 g ($\frac{1}{2}$ oz) flour
35 g ($1\frac{1}{2}$ oz) ground rice
vanilla essence
jam

Line 9 small patty tins with short pastry. Cream the butter and sugar and beat in the egg. Stir in the flour and ground rice. Add

a drop of vanilla. Put a little jam in the bottom of each patty case and half-fill with the mixture. Bake for 15 minutes at 375°F, Gas 5, 190°C.

Apricot Cakes

50 g (2 oz) butter
50 g (2 oz) caster sugar
1 egg
1 heaped tablespoon apricot jam
150 g (6 oz) flour
5 ml (1 teaspoon) baking powder
100 ml (5 fl oz) milk as needed

Cream the butter and sugar. Add the egg and the jam and beat both well in. Stir in the sifted flour and baking powder with enough milk to form a dropping consistency. Stand some paper cake cases in patty tins and half-fill them. Bake at 400°F, Gas 6, 200°C for 10 to 15 minutes.

Raspberry Buns

75 g (3 oz) margarine
150 g (6 oz) self raising flour
pinch salt
50 g (2 oz) caster sugar
1 egg, beaten
raspberry jam

Rub the fat into the flour and salt. Add the sugar. Add the egg to the dry ingredients and mix to form a stiff dough. Form into balls, make a hole and put a little jam in each. Pinch the edges to seal. Turn over and flatten slightly. Brush with milk and dust with sugar. Bake at 425°F, Gas 7, 220°C for 10 minutes. Lower the heat and cook for a few minutes more.

Whipped Walnut Cakes

100 g (4 oz) soft margarine
200 g (8 oz) icing sugar
40 ml (2 dessertspoons) coffee essence
150 g (6 oz) coconut
100 g (4 oz) chopped walnuts

200 g (8 oz) chocolate
half walnuts

Cream the margarine and add the icing sugar and essence. Beat well. Add the coconut and chopped walnuts. Mix well and form into small pyramids using wetted hands. Stand on a wire tray to dry off. Melt the chocolate and have to hand a few half walnuts for topping. Stand the wire tray over a sheet of greaseproof paper to catch the drips. Using a teaspoon coat the pyramids with the chocolate and top each one with a half walnut. When set place in paper cases.

Whipped Walnut Cakes

Nut Cakes

75 g (3 oz) butter
100 g (4 oz) caster sugar
1 egg
drop of vanilla essence
200 g (8 oz) flour
5 ml (1 teaspoon) baking powder
75 g (3 oz) hazelnuts, chopped
little milk

Cream the butter and sugar. Beat in the egg and vanilla and then stir in the flour and baking powder. Stir in the chopped nuts and enough milk to make a dropping consistency. Half-fill some paper cases and stand them in patty tins to keep their shape. Bake for 15 to 20 minutes at 350°F, Gas 4, 180°C.

Eccles Cakes

50 g (2 oz) margarine
50 g (2 oz) demerara sugar
pinch of nutmeg
100 g (4 oz) currants
50 g (2 oz) chopped peel
200 g (½ lb) flaky (page 26) or rough
   puff pastry (page 25)

Melt the margarine and sugar and add the nutmeg and fruit. Roll out the pastry and cut into rounds of about 3 to 4 inches diameter. Put 2 teaspoons of the fruit mix in each round. Bring the pastry over the top of the fruit and join the edges. Turn over and roll lightly until the fruit just shows through the pastry. Make two small slits. Brush with cold water and sprinkle with a little caster sugar. Bake at 425°F, Gas 7, 220°C for 15 to 20 minutes or until browned and risen.

Date Cakes

250 g (10 oz) flour
1 ml (¼ teaspoon) bicarbonate of soda
125 g (5 oz) margarine
200 g (8 oz) dates, chopped finely
125 g (5 oz) sugar
1 egg
milk

Sift the dry ingredients and then rub in the fat. Add the dates and sugar. Beat the egg and add with enough milk to form a stiff dough. Beat well. Drop the mixture into greased patty tins, not more than half full. Bake at 350°F, Gas 4, 180°C for 10 to 15 minutes.

Large Cakes

In this section I have put a number of recipes suited to everyday use. Most of the cakes will keep well, and live up to the name of one of them—cut and come again. . . . Gingerbreads are here; one is a moist gingerbread and one more of a cake, but both will keep well. The ambleside ginger cake is different—a very gingery cake for the many people who like their food hot! Fruit cakes and those with nuts and dates in them also come into this section, and a very nice little cake for a few friends is the gamekeeper's lunch cake taken from an old book which dates from the days when shooting parties were all fed instead of taking their own food. Irish sponge is a lovely light cake which may be filled with jam and whipped cream to delight one and all. The time involved is well rewarded.

There are two basic methods of making sponge cakes; the first requires the creaming of butter and sugar and second is the whisked sponge. For the creaming method, make sure the resulting mix is really very light and fluffy for on this depends the lightness of the cake. And for the whisked sponges the same rule applies—whisk the eggs and sugar until very light indeed. It is best always to sift the dry ingredients over the mix before folding in with a balloon whisk. Most people use a metal spoon, but I have found it quicker and more efficient to use a whisk, and the larger the better.

The recipe for the chocolate cream roll is right . . . there is no flour in it. It is a very rich mixture but surprisingly easy to bring off and most impressive for guests. Children, too, adore it.

Meringue-based cakes again require light handling, and if the sugar is not properly incorporated, the meringue will 'weep' in the baking, leaving caramelly trails round the edges which spoil the appearance entirely.

One or two tips for fruit cakes are worth passing on. Wash and dry the fruit the day before and leave to plump up overnight. Wash glacé cherries, dry well and toss in a little of the measured flour before adding to any of the cake recipes; this will help to prevent the fruit sinking to the bottom of the cake.

Gingerbread

200 g (8 oz) butter
200 g (8 oz) treacle
20 g (8 oz) golden syrup
400 g (1 lb) flour
200 g (8 oz) soft brown sugar
2 ml (½ teaspoon) bicarbonate of soda
15 ml (1 tablespoon) ginger
15 ml (1 tablespoon) mixed spice
70 ml (3 fl oz) or less of milk

Grease and base-line a deep 8-inch cake tin. Warm the butter, treacle and syrup until liquid. Mix the dry ingredients and stir in the melted mixture. Add the milk. Pour into the prepared tin and bake in a slow oven (325°F, Gas 3, 160°C) for 2 hours or until done. *Illustrated in colour between pages 40 and 41.*

Scotch Gingerbread

400 g (1 lb) flour
10 ml (2 teaspoons) ginger
10 ml (2 teaspoons) mixed spice
10 ml (2 teaspoons) cinnamon
200 g (8 oz) soft brown sugar
60 ml (4 tablespoons) black treacle
200 g (8 oz) butter or margarine

100 g (4 oz) stem ginger
2 eggs
5 ml (1 teaspoon) bicarbonate of soda
70 ml (3 fl oz) milk

Mix the dry ingredients with the exception of the bicarbonate of soda. Melt the sugar, treacle and butter or margarine. Chop the ginger into small pieces. Beat the eggs and finally mix the bicarbonate of soda with the milk. Pour the melted ingredients into the sifted flour. Beat in the eggs and stir in the ginger and the bicarbonate of soda last of all. Pour into a greased and lined 8-inch tin and cook in a slow oven (325°F, Gas 3, 160°C) for 2 hours.

Basic Sponge

50 g (2 oz) soft margarine
50 g (2 oz) caster sugar
1 egg
50 g (2 oz) self raising flour

Cream the margarine and sugar and beat in the egg. Fold in the flour and place the mix in a lined, buttered and floured 6-inch tin. Bake at 375°F, Gas 5, 190°C for 25 minutes.

Irish Sponge

5 eggs
200 g (8 oz) caster sugar
150 g (6 oz) flour

Grease, flour and base-line two 8-inch sponge tins. Beat the eggs and caster sugar hard for 10 minutes if using an electric mixer, or for at least 20 minutes if using a balloon whisk. This should produce a very light and pale lemon-coloured mix. Sift the flour over the top and fold in very carefully, still using the balloon whisk. Pour into the prepared tins and bake for 40 minutes at 350°F, Gas 4, 180°C. Turn out and fill as desired. (Very nice with black cherry jam and cream.)

Scotch Sponge

5 eggs
200 g (8 oz) caster sugar
100 g (4 oz) flour
50 g (2 oz) ground almonds

Beat the eggs and sugar until very light and fluffy. Allow a good 10 to 15 minutes. Mix the almonds and flour evenly and fold in using a balloon whisk. Grease and base-line two 8-inch sponge tins and shake the tins with a flour and caster sugar mix to produce a nice crisp edge. Put the mix in these tins and bake for 30 minutes at 375°F, Gas 5, 190°C. Turn out of the tins carefully. Fill with whipped cream and kirsch-soaked pineapple.

Bristol Sponge

100 ml (4 fl oz) water
200 g (8 oz) caster sugar
5 egg yolks

50 g (2 oz) butter
4 egg whites
150 g (6 oz) flour

Squeaky Sponge

3 eggs, separated
150 g (6 oz) caster sugar
pinch of salt
75 g (3 oz) flour

Put the water and sugar in a strong pan and boil for 2 minutes. Cool. Beat the syrup into the egg yolks and continue to beat until the mixture is very thick indeed. This is best done with an electric hand beater and will take a good 8 to 10 minutes. Melt the butter but do not overheat. Whisk the whites and sift the flour. Fold the flour, butter and finally the egg whites into the creamy mixture using a balloon whisk. Pour into a buttered and floured 8-inch cake tin and bake for 40 minutes at 350°F, Gas 4, 180°C. Turn on to a wire rack to cool.

Butter an 8-inch cake tin and sprinkle with caster sugar. Turn out any excess sugar. Beat the yolks and the sugar until thick and creamy. Stiffly beat the whites with a pinch of salt. Sift the flour over the yolk mix and fold in using a balloon whisk. With the same whisk fold in the egg whites. Pour into the prepared cake tin and bake in a moderately hot oven (350°F, Gas 4, 180°C) for 45 minutes.

Bristol Sponge with Heavenly Filling

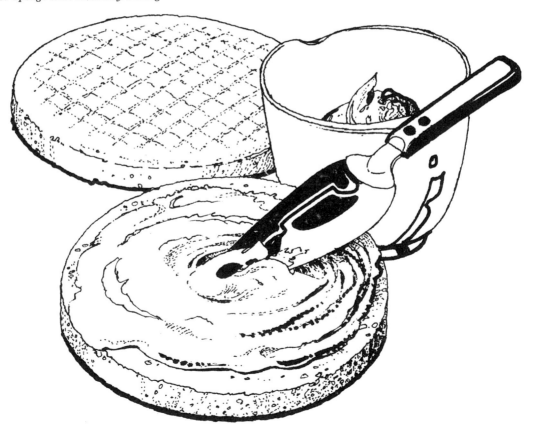

Special Orange Cake

150 g (6 oz) soft margarine
150 g (6 oz) sugar
150 g (6 oz) self raising flour
3 eggs
10 ml (2 tablespoons) milk
7.5 ml (1½ teaspoons) baking powder
grated rind of 2 oranges

Syrup

100 g (4 oz) caster sugar
juice of 2 oranges
30 ml (2 tablespoons) orange liqueur

Topping

100 g (4 oz) plain chocolate
25 g (1 oz) butter

Put all the ingredients for the cake mix into a mixer bowl and beat at high speed for no more than three minutes. Pour into a greased and lined 2 lb loaf tin and bake at 350°F, Gas 4, 180°C for 1 to 1½ hours. Do not open the oven door until the first hour is over or it will sink in the middle. Boil the sugar and the juice for the syrup together for a few minutes and add the orange liqueur. Make some slits with a pointed knife and while the cake is still warm pour the syrup slowly over the top until it is all absorbed. When cold, melt the chocolate with the butter and pour over the top of the cake, allowing it to flow over the edges of the cake in random fashion.

Orange Cake

75 g (3 oz) caster sugar
75 g (3 oz) butter
2 eggs
50 g (2 oz) flour
50 g (2 oz) ground almonds
rind of one orange
1 ml (¼ teaspoon) baking powder

Filling

juice of 1 orange
50 g (2 oz) ground almonds
75 g (3 oz) icing sugar

Cream the sugar and fat until very light. Beat in the eggs one at a time and then lightly add the flour and the almonds with the finely grated orange rind and baking powder. Bake in a greased and base-lined 7-inch cake tin at 350°F, Gas 4, 180°C for 45 minutes. Turn out and when cold cut in layers. Beat the ingredients for the filling together and spread between the layers. Top if liked with a dusting of icing sugar.

Ambleside Gingercake

500 g (1¼ lb) flour
10 ml (2 teaspoons) baking powder
25 g (1 oz) ground ginger
100 g (4 oz) lard
75 g (3 oz) mixed peel

125 g (5 oz) demerara sugar
200 g (8 oz) golden syrup
150 ml (5 fl oz) milk
1 egg

Mix the dry ingredients and rub in the lard. Add the chopped peel and the sugar. Warm the syrup and the milk very gently and take off the heat. Add to a well-beaten egg. Mix into the dry ingredients and combine well. Grease and line an 8-inch square tin and pour in the gingercake mix. Bake at 350°F, Gas 4, 180°C for 1 hour or until done. Cool on a wire tray and cut into small squares.

Angel Cake

50 g (2 oz) flour
165 g (6½ oz) caster sugar
6 egg whites
pinch of salt
3 ml (¾ teaspoon) cream of tartar
2 drops vanilla essence
2 drops almond essence

Sift the flour with 80 g (3½ oz) of the sugar three times to make sure there is plenty of air incorporated. Whisk the egg whites, salt and cream of tarter until foamy. Add the balance of the sugar a tablespoon at a time beating all the time. Also add the essences. Beat until the meringue stands in peaks when the whisk is lifted out. Sift the flour and sugar mix over the meringue and fold in carefully using a balloon whisk. Put the mixture carefully into a clean and dry 7- to 8-inch tube tin. Put in the oven at 375°F, Gas 5, 190°C for 30 minutes. Turn

upside down on a wire tray and leave to cool. When it is cold the cake should drop out of the tin quite cleanly. If it does not do so you can encourage it with a broad bladed knife taken round the outside edge and very carefully round the tube. Decorate as desired with whipped cream and with cherries, angelica or fresh strawberries if in season. *Illustrated in colour opposite page 89.*

Gâteau Miserable

250 g (10 oz) almonds
175 g (7 oz) sugar
75 g (3 oz) self raising flour
8 egg whites
salt

Buttercream

½ cup cold coffee
5 ml (1 teaspoon) instant coffee
5 egg yolks
45 ml (3 tablespoons) sugar
200 g (8 oz) butter

Chop the almonds finely and mix them in with the flour and sugar. Whisk the egg whites stiff and fold in the nut mixture. Butter and line a 10-inch by 6-inch by 2-inch tin or a 10-inch springform tin and pour the mixture into it. Bake at 350°F, Gas 4, 180°C for 20 minutes at the bottom of the oven and then 20 minutes at the top. Cool for 5 minutes in the tin before turning out and carefully removing the paper. Cool. For the icing combine the coffee, instant coffee, egg yolks and sugar in a double boiler and cook, stirring all the time until thick enough to coat the back of the spoon. Soften the butter but do not let it melt. Beat the butter in by the tablespoon with the custard mix over ice. Beat the mix until it holds peaks when the mixer is lifted out. Chill. Split the cake in two and fill with the icing piped in neat rows. Dust the top with icing sugar. (This icing is very difficult to achieve satisfactorily.)

400°F, Gas 6, 200°C for 20 to 25 minutes. Turn out on to a wire tray to cool. Spread the bottom of one cake with lemon curd and put the other one on top. Beat the egg white and stir in the icing sugar to form a stiff paste. Beat well. Put in a bag with a small star pipe and pipe a trellis across the cake and round the edges. Fill each space with a little lemon curd.

Lemon Curd Cake

4 eggs
100 g (4 oz) caster sugar
100 g (4 oz) flour
lemon curd
100 g (4 oz) icing sugar
little egg white

Whisk the eggs and sugar until very thick. Fold in the flour using a balloon whisk and put the mixture into two 8-inch greased and base-lined sandwich tins. Bake at

Sand Cake

50 g (2 oz) flour
50 g (2 oz) ground rice
100 g (4 oz) cornflour
1 ml (¼ teaspoon) baking powder
200 g (8 oz) butter
200 g (8 oz) sugar
rind of 1 lemon
2 eggs

Grease and line an 8-inch cake tin. Sift the flours and baking powder. Cream the

Lemon Curd Cake

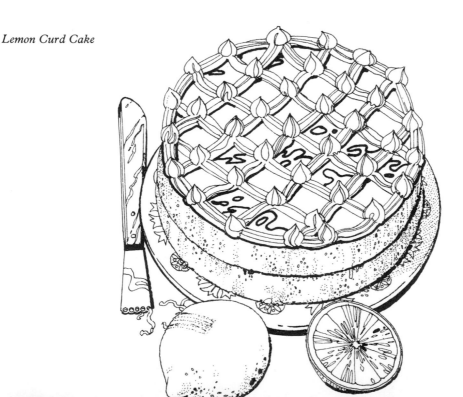

butter and sugar until very light. Beat in the lemon rind and eggs. Beat well in before folding in the flours. Bake for 1 to $1\frac{1}{4}$ hours at 350°F, Gas 4, 180°C. Cool on a wire tray.

Marsala Tangerine Cake

100 g (4 oz) butter
150 g (6 oz) sugar
2 eggs
75 g (3 oz) raisins
50 g (2 oz) almonds
grated rind of 3 tangerines
5 ml (1 teaspoon) vanilla essence
300 g (12 oz) flour
5 ml (1 teaspoon) bicarbonate of soda
2.5 ml ($\frac{1}{2}$ teaspoon) salt
200 ml (6 fl oz) sour milk

Icing

75 g (3 oz) butter
150 g (6 oz) icing sugar
marsala

Topping

75 ml (3 fl oz) water
50 g (2 oz) sugar
50 ml (2 fl oz) marsala
3 tangerines peeled and cleared of pith

Cream fat and sugar well. Stir in the beaten eggs. Add the raisins, chopped almonds, rinds and vanilla. Stir in the dry ingredients and the sour milk. Butter and flour a 9-inch square tin and pour in the mix. Cook at 350°F, Gas 4, 180°C for 30 to 40 minutes. Cool and ice. For the icing cream the butter and add the sugar. Beat in enough marsala to form a spreading consistency. Make a syrup with the water, sugar and marsala. Poach the tangerine pieces for 10 minutes in the syrup. Drain and cool. Pour any remaining syrup over the cake. Fill and top with the icing and decorate with the tangerines.

Pineapple Layer Cake

5 eggs
150 g (6 oz) caster sugar
100 g (4 oz) butter
200 g (8 oz) flour
pinch of salt
pineapple essence or kirsch

Filling

1 cup ratafia crumbs
1 cup whipped cream
1 cup chopped pineapple
2 ml ($\frac{1}{4}$ teaspoon) kirsch
30 ml (4 tablespoons) caster sugar

To make the cake beat the eggs slightly. Add sugar and beat over hot water until very light. Melt butter and fold it in along with the flour and salt, using a balloon whisk. Add a drop of pineapple essence or kirsch. Butter and base-line two 8-inch sandwich tins and cook the mixture in these for 30 minutes at 350°F, Gas 4, 180°C. Turn out and cool on a wire rack. To make the filling, fold the crumbs and pineapple into the sweetened and flavoured whipped cream and use to fill and top the cake. Alternatively, chop and drain an 8 oz can of pineapple. Thicken juice with 1 teaspoon arrowroot and flavour with 1 teaspoon kirsch. This may be used as a filling. In each case top the cake with whipped cream and decorate with cherries.

Spice Cake with Fudge Icing

200 g (8 oz) margarine
200 g (8 oz) soft brown sugar
4 eggs
200 g (8 oz) flour
50 g (2 oz) ground almonds
3 ml ($\frac{3}{4}$ teaspoon) ground cloves
2.5 ml ($\frac{1}{2}$ teaspoon) ground cinnamon
1 ml ($\frac{1}{4}$ teaspoon) bicarbonate of soda

Icing

1 small tin condensed milk
50 g (2 oz) margarine
200 g (8 oz) granulated sugar
vanilla essence

Cream margarine and sugar thoroughly. Beat in the eggs and add the sifted dry ingredients. Grease and line an 8-inch cake tin and pour the mixture in. Bake for $1\frac{3}{4}$ hours at 350°F, Gas 4, 180°C. Turn out. Strip off paper and cool on a wire rack. Put the condensed milk, margarine and sugar in a heavy-based pan. Stir over a low heat until sugar has dissolved. Stir to a golden brown or until a soft ball on the sugar thermometer. Take off the fire and add the vanilla. Beat until it starts to thicken and pour quickly over the cake. Allow to set.

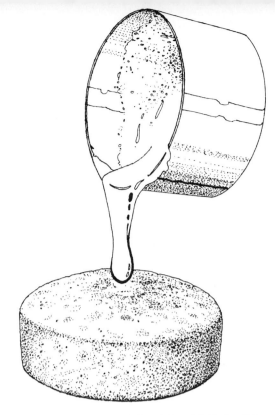

Spice Cake with Fudge Icing

Nursery Layer Cake

200 g (8 oz) butter
200 g (8 oz) caster sugar
3 eggs
300 g (12 oz) self-raising flour
pink colouring
15 ml (1 tablespoon) cocoa

Cream butter and sugar very lightly. Beat in the eggs one at a time with a tablespoon of flour. Fold in the rest of the flour and divide the mixture into three. Make the first part pink. Add a tablespoon of cocoa to another part and leave the last part plain. Cook in three greased and lined 8-inch sandwich tins at 350°F, Gas 4, 180°C for approximately 35–40 minutes or until cooked. Layer up with chocolate butter icing (page 105).

Madeira Cake

225 g (9 oz) butter
225 g (9 oz) caster sugar
8 eggs, separated
sherry glass of whisky
5 ml (1 teaspoon) lemon juice
225 g (9 oz) flour
7.5 ml (1½ teaspoons) baking powder

Cream the butter and sugar very well and then beat in the yolks. Stir in the whisky and lemon juice. Beat in the flour and baking powder. Have the whites stiffly beaten and fold them into the mixture. Turn the mix into a buttered and bottom-lined 8-inch cake tin. Bake in a moderate oven (350°F, Gas 4, 180°C) for 1 hour 40 minutes. Cool for a few minutes in the tin before turning out on to a wire tray to cool completely.

Coconut Cake

3 eggs, separated
100 g (4 oz) butter
225 g (9 oz) sugar
½ kilo (1 lb) flour
10 ml (2 teaspoons) baking powder
25 g (1 oz) almonds
100 ml (3 fl oz) milk
5 ml (1 teaspoon) vanilla essence
75 g (3 oz) coconut

Icing

225 g (9 oz) sugar
100 ml (3 fl oz) water
2.5 ml (½ teaspoon) cream of tartar
6 egg whites
vanilla essence
almond essence

Make the cake by beating the egg whites until stiff. Cream butter and sugar and add yolks. Beat them in. Sift dry ingredients and add with the milk. Beat well before folding in the egg whites and coconut. Cook in two 8-inch greased and floured sandwich tins for 25 minutes at 350°F, Gas 4, 180°C. When cooked, cool on a rack. Make the icing by putting sugar, water and cream of tartar into a pan. Stir over a low heat until sugar has dissolved and bring to a boil. Boil until thick or 228° on a sugar thermometer. Beat egg whites until stiff. Pour mixture on, beating all the time and flavour with a teaspoon each of vanilla and almond essence. Use to fill the cake and to cover the top and sides. Decorate edge with a ring of browned coconut.

Lemon Pavlova

3 egg whites
pinch of salt
150 g (6 oz) caster sugar
15 ml (1 tablespoon) cornflour
5 ml (1 teaspoon) vinegar

Topping

3 egg yolks
75 g (3 oz) caster sugar
zest and juice of a lemon

To decorate

whipped cream
browned flaked almonds

Line a baking sheet with bakewell paper and mark out a 7-inch ring. Turn the paper upside down otherwise the pencil mark will come on to the pavlova. Whisk the whites with salt until stiff. Add sugar, cornflour and vinegar and mix in with a balloon whisk. Turn on to the ring marked on the paper and leaving a hole in the middle, build up the sides gradually. Bake at 325°F, Gas 3, 160°C for ¾ hour. Turn oven off and leave pavlova in for a further ½ hour. Beat the yolks with sugar until creamy and light. Add the zest and juice of a lemon. Cook over a gentle heat until the mixture thickens. Cool. Spread on top of the pavlova and top with whipped cream and browned flaked almonds.

Almond Macaroon Cake

100 g (4 oz) butter
100 g (4 oz) caster sugar
2 eggs
1 yolk
125 g (5 oz) flour
100 g (4 oz) currants
100 g (4 oz) sultanas
100 g (4 oz) angelica
30 g (1½ oz) ground almonds

Macaroon

1 egg white
100 g (4 oz) caster sugar

75 g (3 oz) ground almonds
almond essence
25 g (1 oz) flaked almonds

Line an 8-inch cake tin. Cream the butter and sugar and beat in the eggs and yolk alternately with the flour. Beat well. Stir in the fruits and the ground almonds. For the macaroon mix, half-whip the egg white and stir in the sugar and ground almonds with a drop of essence. Put the cake mix in the prepared tin and spread over the macaroon mix carefully. Sprinkle with the flaked almonds. Cover with a sheet of paper and bake at 350°F, Gas 4, 180°C for about 2 hours. The cover may be taken off in the last half hour to induce the cake to brown nicely on top.

Spice Cake

100 g (4 oz) butter
300 g (12 oz) sugar
3 eggs, separated
5 ml (1 teaspoon) vanilla essence
300 g (12 oz) flour
30 ml (2 tablespoons) cocoa
15 ml (1 tablespoon) cinnamon and cloves
5 ml (1 teaspoon) baking soda
200 ml (6 fl oz) buttermilk

Icing

300 g (12 oz) soft brown sugar
200 ml (6 fl oz) buttermilk
150 g (6 oz) butter
5 ml (1 teaspoon) baking soda
5 ml (1 teaspoon) vanilla essence

To make the cake cream the fat and sugar well. Beat in the yolks and vanilla. Sift dry ingredients and fold in with the milk. Beat well. Stiffly beat the egg whites and fold them into the mixture. Turn into two 9-inch sandwich tins buttered and bottom-lined. Bake at 350°F, Gas 4, 180°C for about 40 minutes. Cool on a wire tray. Put all the ingredients for the icing into a heavy pan and cook over a low heat, to 236° on a sugar thermometer (soft ball). Take off the heat and beat until it is of a dropping consistency. Fill the cake with about one third and use the rest to cover the top and sides, using a wet spatula to make it smooth.

Turkish Nut Cake

Turkish Nut Cake

9 eggs, separated
225 g (9 oz) sugar
grated rind of a lemon
pinch of salt
25 g (1 oz) rice flour
100 g (4 oz) flour
100 g (4 oz) butter

Syrup

600 ml (1 pint) water
350 g (14 oz) icing sugar
45 ml (3 tablespoons) lemon juice
4 whole cloves
strip of lemon rind

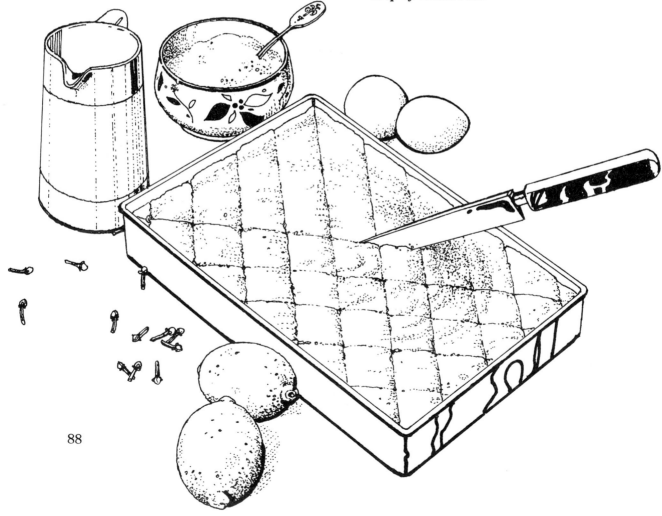

Northern Fruitcake

*Russian Walnut Cake (left) and Old-fashioned Coffee
Cake*

Angel Cake (front) and Devil's Food Cake

Beat egg yolks with sugar and rind until very thick and lemon coloured. Beat egg whites with a pinch of salt until stiff but not dry. Sift dry ingredients. Melt the butter. Fold these in alternately using a wire whisk. Turn into a buttered 13-inch by 9-inch by 2-inch baking tin. Bake at 350°F, Gas 4, 180°C for 45 to 50 minutes. Cool in tin. Put all the ingredients for the syrup into a heavy pan. Dissolve sugar gently and bring to the boil stirring all the time. Boil without stirring for 10 minutes. Strain. Cut the cake into diagonal pieces and make into a diamond shape. Pour the hot syrup evenly over the cake. Allow to stand until the liquid is absorbed and the cake is completely cooled. This looks very plain but is delicious.

Plain Plum Cake

200 g (8 oz) flour
1 ml (¼ teaspoon) ground cloves
1 ml (¼ teaspoon) cinnamon
50 g (2 oz) raisins
50 g (2 oz) currants
glacé cherries
100 g (4 oz) butter
100 g (4 oz) caster sugar
2 eggs
5 ml (1 teaspoon) baking powder
milk

Sift the flour and mix with the spices and fruit. Cream the butter and sugar thoroughly and add the eggs alternately with the flour mixture. Add the baking powder with the last spoon of the flour and sufficient milk to form a dropping consistency. Bake in a lined deep cake tin in a hot oven for 20 minutes until set

(400°F, Gas 6, 200°C) and reduce the heat to 350°F, Gas 4, 180°C for 1½ hours. Leave in the tin for a few minutes before turning out onto a wire tray to cool.

Burnt House Cake

200 g (8 oz) butter
200 g (8 oz) sugar
5 ml (1 teaspoon) bicarbonate of soda
125 ml (5 fl oz) milk
150 g (6 oz) ground rice
250 g (10 oz) flour
15 ml (1 tablespoon) mixed spice
200 g (8 oz) raisins
200 g (8 oz) sultanas

Cream the butter and sugar. Mix the bicarbonate of soda with the milk and add alternately with the sifted dry ingredients and the fruit to the creamed mixture. Bake in a buttered and lined 8-inch cake tin in a moderate oven (350°F, Gas 4, 180°C) for 2½ hours. Cool for a few minutes in the tin before turning onto a wire rack.

Dundee Cake

150 g (6 oz) flour
pinch salt
2.5 ml (½ teaspoon) baking powder
100 g (4 oz) butter
75 g (3 oz) caster sugar
3 eggs
5 ml (1 teaspoon) treacle
50 g (2 oz) sultanas
50 g (2 oz) citron peel
200 g (8 oz) currants
25 g (1 oz) almonds

Sift the flour, salt, and baking powder. Cream the butter and sugar until light. Add 1 tablespoon of the flour and one egg and beat very well. Repeat with the other eggs and then add the treacle. Mix the rest of the flour with the fruit and add. Turn into a 7-inch lined cake tin. Arrange the almonds all over the top and bake at 350°F, Gas 4, 180°C for 1½ to 2 hours.

Almond Cake de luxe

200 g (8 oz) butter or margarine
200 g (8 oz) sugar
4 eggs
almond essence
vanilla essence
200 g (8 oz) flour
2.5 ml (½ teaspoon) baking powder
flaked almonds

Filling

100 g (4 oz) ground almonds
50 g (2 oz) caster sugar
40 g (1½ oz) icing sugar
little egg to bind

Line an 8-inch cake tin. Make the filling by mixing the almonds and sugars and binding with some egg. Roll out so that it will fit the base of the cake tin but do not put it in yet. Cream the butter and sugar for the cake and beat in the eggs one at a time. Add a little vanilla and almond essence and sift in the flour and baking powder. Spread half of this cake mix in the bottom of the cake tin and carefully ease in the almond paste layer. Top with the rest of the cake mix and some flaked almonds and bake at 350°F, Gas 4, 180°C for 1¼ to 1½ hours.

Bride Cake

300 g (12 oz) butter
300 g (12 oz) soft brown sugar
6 eggs
15 ml (1 tablespoon) milk
15 ml (1 tablespoon) black treacle
400 g (1 lb) currants
400 g (1 lb) raisins
200 g (8 oz) mixed peel
400 g (1 lb) flour
5 ml (1 teaspoon) baking powder
50 g (2 oz) ground almonds

Almond Cake de luxe

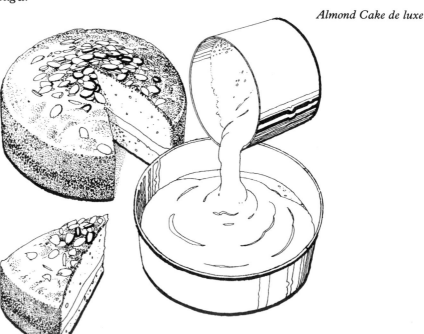

Cream the butter and sugar together until light. Add the eggs one at a time and beat in thoroughly. A tablespoon of flour may be added with each egg to prevent curdling. Heat the milk and treacle and add to the creamed mix with the fruit and with the rest of the flour and baking powder mixed. Add ground almonds. Bake in a 10-inch lined and buttered tin for $3\frac{1}{2}$ to 4 hours at 350°F, Gas 4, 180°C. Cool in the tin for 10 to 15 minutes before turning out to cool completely on a wire tray. Wrap in greaseproof paper and tinfoil and allow to rest for 6 weeks before cutting.

Northern Fruitcake

$\frac{1}{2}$ kilo (1 lb) citron peel
200 g (8 oz) glacé cherries
200 g (8 oz) glacé pineapple
2 kilo (4 lb) raisins
1 cup whisky
$\frac{1}{2}$ kilo (1 lb) blanched split almonds
45 ml (3 tablespoons) rosewater
$\frac{1}{2}$ kilo (1 lb) butter
350 g (14 oz) sugar
12 eggs, separated
25 g (1 oz) chocolate
50 ml (3 fl oz) Glayva
15 ml (1 tablespoon) each of allspice,
   nutmeg, cinnamon
5 ml (1 teaspoon) ground cloves
$\frac{1}{2}$ jar cranberry jelly
30 ml (2 tablespoons) whisky
$\frac{1}{2}$ kilo (1 lb) walnuts
$\frac{1}{2}$ kilo (1 lb) flour

Chop the citron peel finely and quarter the cherries. Chop the glacé pineapple and mix the fruits. Add the whisky and allow to stand for 12 hours. Add rosewater to split almonds and stand for 12 hours. Cream butter and add sugar and cream well. Beat in the yolks of the eggs. Melt chocolate. Whip egg whites stiff. Add Glayva and spices to the yolk mix and beat in. Add jelly, chocolate and whisky. Fold in whites with sifted flour and then add fruit, walnuts and almonds. Butter and line three 9-inch by 5-inch by 3-inch cake tins and fill the mixture into them. Level the cake and put in a moderate oven (375°F, Gas 5, 190°C) for 3 hours. Cool in tin for the first 30 minutes and turn out then to complete the cooling on a wire rack. Wrap in a whisky-soaked cloth, or if preferred a sheet of greaseproof paper and overwrap in both cases with tin foil, or put in a tin. Store a month before using. *Illustrated in colour opposite page 88.*

Cut and Come Again Cake

400 g (1 lb) flour
10 ml (2 teaspoons) baking powder
200 g (8 oz) sugar
75 g (3 oz) lard
75 g (3 oz) butter
200 g (8 oz) sultanas
150 g (6 oz) currants
2 eggs
milk

Mix all the dry ingredients and rub in the fats. Mix in the fruits. Beat the eggs lightly and stir into the cake. Add a little milk if it is required and put the mixture into a lined 8-inch deep cake tin. Bake at 350°F, Gas 4, 180°C for 1 hour. Test with a skewer to see if it is cooked through before turning out on a wire tray to cool.

Hungarian Cake

200 g (8 oz) chocolate
150 g (6 oz) sugar
125 g (5 oz) ground walnuts
50 g (2 oz) cake crumbs
8 egg whites
300 ml (½ pint) double cream
100 g (4 oz) chocolate
little water

Melt 200 g (8 oz) chocolate over hot water. Stir in sugar, ground nuts, cake crumbs and lightly beaten egg whites. Mix well. Butter two 8-inch sandwich tins and put the mixture in. Bake at 250°F, Gas ½, 130°C until set and golden, approximately 1 to 1½ hours. Cool on a wire rack. Whip the cream and spread on one layer of the cake. Top with the other layer. Melt the 100 g (4 oz) chocolate with a little water and spread over the top.

Cherry Pineapple Cake

150 g (6 oz) butter or margarine
150 g (6 oz) sugar
3 eggs
50 g (2 oz) glacé cherries
50 g (2 oz) glacé pineapple
50 g (2 oz) angelica
125 g (5 oz) flour
5 ml (1 teaspoon) baking powder
50 g (2 oz) ground almonds

Grease and line an eight-inch cake tin. Cream the butter and sugar and beat in the eggs. Wash, chop and dry the fruit and add to it two spoons of the measured flour. Add the rest of the flour and baking powder to the mix, and finally the fruits and ground almonds. Bake in the prepared tin for 50 to 60 minutes at 350°F, Gas 4, 180°C. Cool on a wire tray and top with American frosting (see page 106). Decorate with bits of angelica and glacé cherries.

Nut Cake

200 g (8 oz) ground hazelnuts
200 g (8 oz) caster sugar
5 ml (1 teaspoon) cinnamon
5 eggs, separated
small cup honey
300 ml (½ pint) double cream
apricot jam

Mix together the nuts, sugar and cinnamon. Stir in the beaten yolks and the very slightly warmed honey. Beat the egg whites very stiff and fold in carefully. Butter and flour two 8-inch cake tins and pour in the mixture. Bake at 325°F, Gas 3, 160°C until firm. Fill with whipped unsweetened cream, and apricot jam.

Date Cake

100 g (4 oz) butter or margarine
100 g (4 oz) sugar
200 g (8 oz) dates
200 g (8 oz) flour
5 ml (1 teaspoon) bicarbonate of soda
150 ml (6 fl oz) milk

Cream the butter or margarine and sugar very thoroughly. Chop the dates and mix with the flour. Dissolve the baking soda in the milk and beat in with the flour and dates. Bake in a lined 7-inch cake tin for about 2 hours at 350°F, Gas 4, 180°C.

Wardley Cake

200 g (8 oz) butter
300 ml (½ pint) milk
200 g (8 oz) ground rice
200 g (8 oz) self raising flour
200 g (8 oz) caster sugar
15 ml (3 teaspoons) baking powder
200 g (8 oz) glacé ginger
200 g (8 oz) glacé cherries

Warm the butter and the milk. Mix all the dry ingredients and add the chopped glacé ginger and glacé cherries both washed and patted dry. Mix the butter and milk into the cake and bake in a greased and lined cake tin. Bake at 325°F, Gas 3, 160°C for 3 to 4 hours.

Gamekeeper's Lunch Cake

100 g (4 oz) butter
100 g (4 oz) caster sugar
2 eggs
30 ml (2 tablespoons) milk
200 g (8 oz) flour
10 ml (2 teaspoons) baking powder
2.5 (½ teaspoon) cinnamon
50 g (2 oz) currants
50 g (2 oz) raisins

Grease and line a deep 6-inch cake tin. Cream the butter and sugar and beat in the eggs very thoroughly. Stir in the sifted flour, baking powder, spice, fruits and milk. Turn into the tin and bake at 350°F, Gas 4, 180°C for 45 to 50 minutes. Leave in the tin for a few minutes before turning out onto a wire tray to cool.

Russian Walnut Cake

150 g (6 oz) walnuts
50 g (2 oz) mixed peel
5 eggs, separated
165 g (7 oz) caster sugar
15 ml (1 tablespoon) lemon juice
50 g (2 oz) flour
2.5 ml (½ teaspoon) salt
300 ml (½ pint) double cream
2.5 ml (½ teaspoon) vanilla essence
150 ml (4 oz) black cherry jam

Grate the nuts coarsely or put them for a few moments in a blender. Chop the peel very finely. Beat egg whites until stiff. Add 75 g (3 oz) of the sugar and whisk again, forming a stiff meringue. In a small bowl beat the yolks and lemon juice until thick and yellow. Beat in 75 g of sugar. Add the peel and nuts. Using a balloon whisk fold this mixture into the egg whites, with the flour and salt. Turn into a buttered and lined 9-inch by 9-inch tin. Bake at 325°F, Gas 3, 160°C for 45 minutes. Cool in tin and turn out very carefully. Peel off the paper. Beat the double cream with the rest of the sugar and flavour with vanilla. Pipe a decorative edge and a lattice across the top. Fill each of the squares so formed with a teaspoon of cherry jam. *Illustrated in colour between pages 88 and 89.*

Winter Cake

400 g (1 lb) flour
15 ml (1 tablespoon) ground ginger
2.5 ml (½ teaspoon) bicarbonate of soda
200 g (8 oz) dark brown sugar
300 ml (½ pint) milk
25 g (1 oz) citron peel
200 g (8 oz) butter
4 eggs
400 g (1 lb) treacle
whole blanched almonds

Mix the dry ingredients. Warm the milk and in it melt the butter. Beat the eggs in a bowl with the treacle. Add the eggs to the milk mixture and then stir it into the dry mixture. Beat well. Bake in a 9-inch square tin with the almonds placed on top for 45 minutes to an hour at 375°F, Gas 5, 190°C.

Special Date Cake

4 egg yolks
100 g (4 oz) sugar
200 g (8 oz) stoned chopped dates
150 g (6 oz) chopped almonds
4 egg whites
300 ml (½ pint) double cream
vanilla and sugar

Beat the egg yolks with 75 g (3 oz) sugar until very thick. Fold in the dates and almonds and mix well. Stiffly beat the egg whites. Add rest of sugar and beat again. Fold into the date mixture and turn into a

buttered and floured 8-inch cake tin. Cook at 375°F, Gas 5, 190°C for 30 minutes. Cool on a wire rack. Cut in two and fill with whipped sweetened cream flavoured with vanilla.

Cherry Cake

150 g (6 oz) margarine
150 g (6 oz) caster sugar
3 eggs
150 g (6 oz) flour
pinch salt
5 ml (1 teaspoon) baking powder
50 g (2 oz) ground almonds
150 g (6 oz) glacé cherries

Cream the fat and sugar and add the eggs one at a time, beating well. Stir in the flour, salt, baking powder and the ground almonds. Wash the cherries and dry on a paper towel. Halve them and stir in with a little of the flour at the last moment. Cook in a lined 6-inch cake tin for 1 hour at 350°F, Gas 4, 180°C. Then turn the heat down to 325°F, Gas 3, 170°C for about 30 minutes until cooked through.

Date Nut Chocolate Cake

200 g (8 oz) dates
7.5 ml (¾ teaspoon) bicarbonate of soda
50 ml (2 fl oz) hot water
100 g (4 oz) butter
225 g (9 oz) sugar
75 g (3 oz) chocolate
5 ml (1 teaspoon) vanilla essence

175 g (7 oz) flour
2.5 ml (½ teaspoon) baking powder
2.5 ml (½ teaspoon) salt
50 g (2 oz) walnuts
2 eggs
100 ml (4 fl oz) sour cream

Butter and flour two 8-inch cake tins. Chop the dates and put them in a pan with the bicarbonate of soda and add the water. Stand on one side. Cream the butter and sugar, and melt the chocolate and allow to cool slightly. Add the vanilla essence. Sift the dry ingredients and chop the walnuts. Beat eggs and chocolate into the creamed mix. Fold in dry ingredients with the sour cream and then stir in the dates. Pour in tins. Sprinkle the nuts over the top and bake at 350°F, Gas 4, 180°C for 50 minutes. Cool on racks. Drip 50 g (2 oz) of melted chocolate over the top as decoration.

Children's Cake

200 g (8 oz) butter
200 g (8 oz) caster sugar
4 eggs
200 g (8 oz) flour
200 g (8 oz) glacé cherries
25 g (1 oz) pistachios
25 g (1 oz) chopped almonds
rind of 1 lemon

Cream the butter and sugar well together and beat in the eggs one at a time with a little of the flour with each one. Wash the cherries, halve and toss in a little of the flour. Add the rest of the flour to the creamed mix and finally add the fruit and nuts with the finely grated rind of the lemon. Bake in a lined 8-inch cake tin for 1½ hours at 375°F, Gas 5, 190°C. When cool cover with a soft glacé icing using the juice from the lemon as part of the liquid.

Tipsy Orange Cake

½ kilo (1 lb) butter
300 g (12 oz) sugar
6 eggs, separated
½ kilo (1 lb) flour
10 ml (2 teaspoons) each bicarbonate of
*   soda and baking powder*
350 ml (12 fl oz) sour cream
grated rind of 2 oranges
100 g (4 oz) chopped walnuts
150 ml (5 fl oz) orange juice
150 g (6 oz) sugar
30 ml (2 tablespoons) orange liqueur

Cream the butter and sugar and beat in the egg yolks one at a time. Sift the flour, baking soda, and baking powder together. Add these dry ingredients to the mix alternately with the sour cream. Stir in the orange rind and chopped nuts. Fold in the stiffly-beaten egg whites. Pour into two buttered 9-inch tube tins and bake at 350°F, Gas 4, 180°C for 55 minutes. Meanwhile mix the juice, sugar and liqueur together and boil up for a minute. Pour this syrup gently and evenly all over the cakes while they are still warm. Cool in the tins. Turn out. Serve one with whipped cream or plain and wrap the other one for the freezer, or wrap well in foil. *Illustrated in colour opposite page 8.*

Chocolate Cream Cake

100 g (4 oz) butter
250 g (10 oz) caster sugar
4 eggs, separated
200 g (8 oz) flour
100 ml (½ cup) cocoa
5 ml (1 teaspoon) baking powder
2.5 ml (½ teaspoon) bicarbonate of soda
pinch of salt
200 ml (7 fl oz) milk
5 ml (1 teaspoon) vanilla essence
300 ml (½ pint) double cream
sugar

Cream the butter and sugar until light and beat in the egg yolks one at a time. Sift all the dry ingredients together and add them alternately with the milk and vanilla. Stiffly whip the whites and fold them in carefully. Bake in a lined 8-inch cake tin for an hour at 325°F, Gas 3, 160°C. Test to be sure it is done before turning out on a wire rack to cool. Split in two and fill with whipped sweetened cream. Reassemble the cake and dust over with sifted icing sugar.

Spicy Chocolate Cake

200 g (8 oz) butter
150 g (6 oz) caster sugar
grated rind of a lemon
1 ml (¼ teaspoon) cinnamon
1 ml (¼ teaspoon) cloves
150 g (6 oz) flour
50 g (2 oz) rice flour
150 g (6 oz) chocolate powder

5 eggs
5 ml (1 teaspoon) vanilla essence
10 ml (2 teaspoons) coffee essence
5 ml (1 teaspoon) baking powder

Fudge Icing

75 g (3 oz) soft brown sugar
75 g (3 oz) white fat
45 ml (3 tablespoons) milk
200 g (8 oz) icing sugar
30 ml (2 tablespoons) cocoa

To make the cake cream together the butter, sugar, lemon rind and spices. Beat for 10 minutes. Sift the flour, rice flour and cocoa together and whisk the eggs lightly. Add alternately along with the vanilla and coffee essence and the baking powder and stir well in. Put the mix in a greased and base-lined tin. Bake in a moderate oven (350°F, Gas 4, 180°C) for 1 to 1½ hours. Cool on a wire tray. To make the icing melt the soft brown sugar, fat and milk in a heavy pan. Sift the icing sugar and cocoa and pour in the melted ingredients. Beat well, and use to top the cake.

Devil's Food Cake

150 g (6 oz) flour
5 ml (1 teaspoon) bicarbonate of soda
1 ml (¼ teaspoon) baking powder
pinch of salt
50 g (2 oz) cocoa
150 ml (7 fl oz) water
100 g (4 oz) margarine
250 g (10 oz) caster sugar
2 eggs

Butter and base-line two 8-inch sandwich tins. Sift the flour, bicarbonate of soda and baking powder with the salt. In a jug mix the cocoa with the water. Cream the margarine and add the sugar. Beat well. Add the whisked eggs and beat again. Stir in the cocoa mix and the flour and beat lightly. Pour into the prepared tins and put in a moderate oven (350°F, Gas 4, 180°C) for 30 to 35 minutes. Cool. Fill and top with simple fudge icing (page 106). *Illustrated opposite page 89.*

Chocolate Orange Cake

150 g (6 oz) butter or margarine
150 g (6 oz) sugar
3 eggs
grated rind of 1 orange
150 g (6 oz) flour
5 ml (1 teaspoon) baking powder

Filling

75 g (3 oz) ground almonds
75 g (3 oz) icing sugar
green colouring
orange juice and a little grated rind

Icing

150 g (6 oz) icing sugar
75 g (3 oz) chocolate
15 g (½ oz) butter
little hot water

Make cake by creaming butter and sugar thoroughly. Beat in the eggs and the rind. Fold in the flour and baking powder sifted together. Grease and line two 8-inch sandwich tins and pour in the mixture. Bake in a moderately hot oven (400°F, Gas 6, 200°C) for 25 to 30 minutes. Cool on a wire tray. For the filling mix all ingredients to a firm paste and colour it green. Press it to fit the shape of the cake and use as the filling. For the icing sift the sugar and melt the chocolate with the butter. Stir in the icing sugar and add a little boiling water as necessary to make a dropping consistency. Using a firm spatula spread over the top and sides of the cake. It is useful to have a jug of hot water to dip the spatula into when spreading the icing.

Sacher Torte

125 g (5 oz) butter
125 g (5 oz) icing sugar
6 eggs, separated
125 g (5 oz) chocolate
125 g (5 oz) flour
sieved apricot jam
100 g (4 oz) almonds, browned
chocolate water icing (page 104)

Cream the butter and sugar until very light and fluffy. Whisk the egg whites stiffly. Melt the chocolate over a pan of hot water. Beat the egg yolks into the creamed mix and then the chocolate. Fold the egg whites in, then sift over the flour and fold that in very carefully. Bake in a lined swiss roll tin in a moderately hot oven (350°F, Gas 4, 180°C) for 15 minutes or until set. When cool cut in three strips all the same width and layer with sieved apricot jam. Spread the sides with apricot jam and press on browned almonds. Top with chocolate water icing.

Chocolate Cream Roll

5 eggs
125 g (5 oz) sugar
150 g (6 oz) plain chocolate
45 ml (3 tablespoons) water
25 g (1 oz) browned ground almonds
300 ml (½ pint) double cream
5 ml (1 teaspoon) vanilla essence
grated chocolate

Separate the eggs and beat the yolks with 100 g (4 oz) of the sugar until very thick indeed. Melt the chocolate and water together over a low heat. Beat the egg whites stiff. Stir the chocolate into the egg yolk mix and add the browned almonds. Fold in the egg whites. Have ready a swiss roll tin lined with non-stick paper and the corners carefully mitred. Pour the mix into the paper and bake at 350°F, Gas 4, 180°C for 15 minutes. It will still be a little soft to the touch but do not be alarmed. Cover quickly with a clean tea towel wrung out in cold water, and put right away in the fridge to cool. After 1 hour remove the cloth very carefully. Grate some chocolate all over the top of the cake and put a sheet of non-stick paper on top of this. Cover with a firm board and invert. Remove the tin, which should be clean. Ease off the paper very carefully. Whip the cream with the rest of the sugar and the vanilla. Spread all over the top of the cake and then roll very gently from the long edge using the paper to ease it over, pressing gently if needed to keep in place. Sprinkle with more grated chocolate and lift on to a long dish or cake plate. Serves 10. Very rich and rewarding to make. *Illustrated in colour opposite page 8.*

Super Chocolate Cake

200 g (8 oz) chocolate
200 g (8 oz) butter
7 eggs, separated
15 ml (1 tablespoon) maraschino
75 g (3 oz) flour
100 g (4 oz) ground almonds
200 g (8 oz) caster sugar

Melt the chocolate and beat it with the softened butter. Beat the egg yolks into the butter and chocolate with the maraschino. Sift in the flour and almonds and sugar. Fold the stiffly beaten egg whites into the mixture and put in a lined and buttered 8-inch tin. Bake at 325°F, Gas 3, 160°C for 45 to 50 minutes. Cool on a wire tray and if liked run on a little plain water icing flavoured with maraschino.

Caddiston Cake

150 g (6 oz) butter
150 g (6 oz) demerara sugar
50 g (2 oz) golden syrup
3 eggs
400 g (1 lb) sultanas
100 g (4 oz) mixed peel
1 cup warm milk
300 g (12 oz) flour

Cream the butter and sugar very thoroughly with the syrup. Beat in the eggs with the fruit and the milk. Stir in the flour and put the mix into a lined 8-inch square cake tin. Bake at 325°F, Gas 3, 160°C for 2 hours or until a skewer inserted in the middle comes out clean. Cool for a few minutes in the tin before putting on a wire rack to cool. Wrap in greaseproof paper and foil to keep or else put in an airtight tin. This cake keeps well.

Rich Mocha Gâteau

100 g (4 oz) dark chocolate
200 g (8 oz) butter
4 egg yolks
100 g (4 oz) caster sugar
90 ml (6 tablespoons) Kahlua (coffee-flavoured liqueur)
15 ml (1 tablespoon) Camp coffee essence
2 packets of boudoir biscuits or home made sponge fingers

Melt chocolate and half of the butter slowly. Put sugar and egg yolks in the top of a double boiler and beat over a gentle heat until very thick. Take off the heat and beat in the melted chocolate and the rest of the softened butter. Beat in half of the Kahlua. Mix the Camp coffee essence with 45 ml (3 tablespoons) of water and the rest of the Kahlua. Butter a 2 lb loaf tin. In the bottom pour a thin layer of the chocolate and coffee sauce. Dip the boudoir biscuits or sponge fingers in the Kahlua mixture and lay in rows in the bottom of the tin. Continue in layers of sauce and dipped biscuits until all the mixture is used up. Chill. Dip into very hot water just before turning out. Decorate with whole browned almonds and angelica.

Coffee Meringue Cake

4 egg whites
200 g (8 oz) caster sugar
5 ml (1 teaspoon) instant powdered coffee
30 ml (2 tablespoons) cornflour
300 ml (½ pint) double cream
30 ml (2 tablespoons) Kahlua (coffee-flavoured liqueur)
25 g (1 oz) browned flaked almonds

Whisk the egg whites stiff and whisk in about half the sugar until really stiff. Sift the sugar, coffee and cornflour together and fold into the meringue using a balloon whisk. Mark three 8-inch rings on non-stick paper and put them upside down on baking sheets. Using a large star nozzle and forcing bag pipe three rounds using the pencilled ring as a guide. Decorate the best layer with large stars all round the edge. Bake at 300°F, Gas 2, 150°C for an hour. Cool in the oven. Whip the cream with the Kahlua and pipe some decoratively on the top layer. Spread the remaining cream on the other two layers and place carefully on top of each other. Put the decorated layer on top and decorate further with browned flaked almonds. *Illustrated in colour opposite page 8.*

Old-fashioned Coffee Cake

8 eggs
225 g (9 oz) caster sugar
125 g (5 oz) flour
125 g (5 oz) finely-chopped or nibbed almonds

Filling

6 egg yolks
200 g (8 oz) caster sugar
75 ml (3 fl oz) strong black coffee
150 g (6 oz) butter
vanilla essence
grated chocolate

Separate the eggs and whisk the yolks and sugar together until thick and creamy. Fold in the flour and almonds. Whisk the egg whites very stiffly and fold them into the mix. Pour into three buttered, floured and base-lined 8-inch sandwich tins. Bake at 375°F, Gas 5, 190°C for 15 minutes. Turn out to cool on a wire tray. For the filling beat the yolks and sugar until very thick. Add the coffee and stir over hot water until thick and creamy. Beat until cold, off the heat. Soften the butter but do not melt it. Beat into the egg mixture and finally add the vanilla flavouring. Use to fill top and cover the sides of the cake. Decorate the top edge with some finely-grated chocolate. *Illustrated in colour between pages 88 and 89.*

Coffee Cake (1)

5 eggs, separated
125 g (5 oz) sugar
100 g (4 oz) plain chocolate
5 ml (1 teaspoon) soft breadcrumbs
50 g (2 oz) ground almonds
5 ml (1 teaspoon) pulverised coffee

Filling

3 egg yolks
15 ml (3 teaspoons) icing sugar

100 ml (4 fl oz) strong black coffee
100 g (4 oz) softened butter

Combine the egg yolks and sugar and beat until thick. Soften the chocolate in a bowl over hot water. Fold in the ground almonds, coffee and breadcrumbs. Stiffly beat the egg whites and fold them in also. Butter and flour an 8-inch cake tin and pour the mixture in. Bake at 375°F, Gas 5, 190°C for 25–30 minutes or until done. Cool on a wire rack.

For the filling, beat the egg yolks and combine with sugar and coffee in a double boiler. Stir over a gentle heat until mixture thickens. Beat off the heat until the mixture is smooth and thick. Melt butter and beat in. Slice cake in 2 or 3 layers and fill with this cream. Spread top with icing and garnish with browned almonds.

Coffee Cake (2)

150 g (6 oz) butter
150 g (6 oz) sugar
200 g (8 oz) flour
5 ml (1 teaspoon) baking powder
4 eggs
5 ml (1 teaspoon) coffee essence
2–5 ml (½ teaspoon) vanilla essence

Filling

100 g (4 oz) butter
150 g (6 oz) icing sugar
10 ml (2 teaspoons) coffee essence

Cream butter and sugar well. Beat in the essences and then the eggs one at a time along with the sifted flour and baking powder. Grease and line two 8-inch tins and pour the mixture into these. Bake at 375°F, Gas 5, 190°C for 25 to 30 minutes until firm. Cool on a wire tray. Make the filling by creaming the butter and sugar and adding the essence. Put in between the two halves of the cake. Dust the top with a little icing sugar.

Mrs. MacFadden's Coffee Cake

100 g (4 oz) self raising flour
25 g (1 oz) instant coffee powder

100 g (4 oz) soft margarine
125 g (5 oz) caster sugar
2 eggs
5 ml (1 teaspoon) milk

Line and grease an 8-inch sandwich tin. Put all the ingredients into the bowl at once and beat for 3 to 4 minutes until light and well-mixed. It is best to use an electric hand whisk for this. Put the mix into the prepared tin and put in the oven at 375°F, Gas 5, 190°C for 35 minutes. Turn out on a wire rack and spread with a good layer of coffee butter icing (see page 104). Decorate.

Mrs MacFadden's Coffee Cake

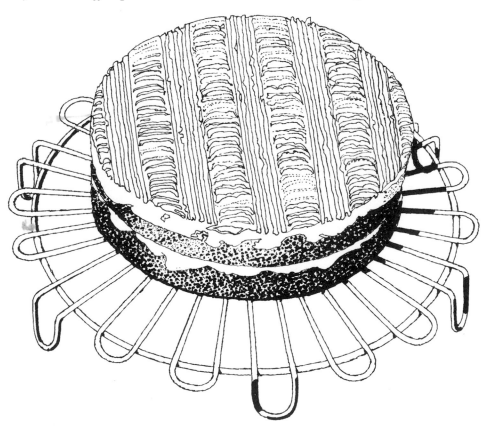

Icings & Fillings

This is only a small selection of the icings that are available to put the finishing touch to your cakes and biscuits. There are endless variations and there are many other recipes in the cake sections. Try using some of these with other cakes. One thing to remember is that it is unwise to try and put a heavy icing on a light cake, for it will drag the cake apart in the application. Putting icings on is a matter of practice but I have found that the best implement for this is the flexible spatula with a slightly curved blade. As well as spreading icings on the sides and tops of cakes, spatulas are a great boon in other fields of cookery, and can curve nicely down the side of a bowl to scrape it clean. For Royal icings and heavy fondant icings it is best to use a heavy quality plain spatula with a straight edge.

Marshmallow Topping

100 ml (½ cup) milk
3 cups marshmallows
½ teaspoon vanilla essence
300 ml (½ pint) double cream

In a double boiler put the marshmallows and milk and put over hot water to melt. Stir until quite smooth. Add vanilla and chill this mix until it starts to thicken. Whip the cream and fold the marshmallows into it with a balloon whisk. Top and fill an 8-inch cake.

Coffee Butter Icing

100 g (4 oz) butter
75 g (3 oz) icing sugar
75 g (3 oz) caster sugar
10 ml (2 teaspoons) coffee essence

Cream the butter with the two sugars until light. Add the coffee essence and beat well in. Use to top one 8-inch cake.

Five Minute Icing

150 g (6 oz) caster sugar
1 egg white
vanilla essence
30 ml (2 tablespoons) water
1 ml (¼ teaspoon) cream of tartar

Put all the ingredients into a bowl. Stand over a pan of boiling water. Stir until the sugar is dissolved. Whisk fast for 2 to 3 minutes until peaks form. Take off heat and whisk again until the peaks are stiff and the mixture is cold. Swirl on the top and sides of a chocolate layer cake.

Chocolate Water Icing

75 g (3 oz) icing sugar
25 g (1½ oz) chocolate
boiling water

104

Sift the sugar into a bowl. Melt the chocolate and mix in the sugar and enough boiling water to produce a spreading consistency. Use to ice eclairs, jap cakes etc.

Chocolate Butter Icing

100 g (4 oz) butter
150 g (6 oz) icing sugar
50 g (2 oz) chocolate

Cream the butter and sugar well together. Melt the chocolate over a pan of hot water and stir in. Use to top and fill a 7-inch cake.

Maple Syrup Icing

$\frac{3}{4}$ cup maple syrup
$\frac{1}{4}$ cup sugar
1 egg white

Boil the water and syrup in a heavy pan until it registers 260°F on a sugar thermometer, or until it spins a thread. Beat up the egg white and continue to beat while pouring on the syrup in a steady stream. When all the syrup is beaten in continue to beat until the icing thickens to a spreading consistency. This will fill and top a 9-inch sponge cake.

Maple Syrup Icing

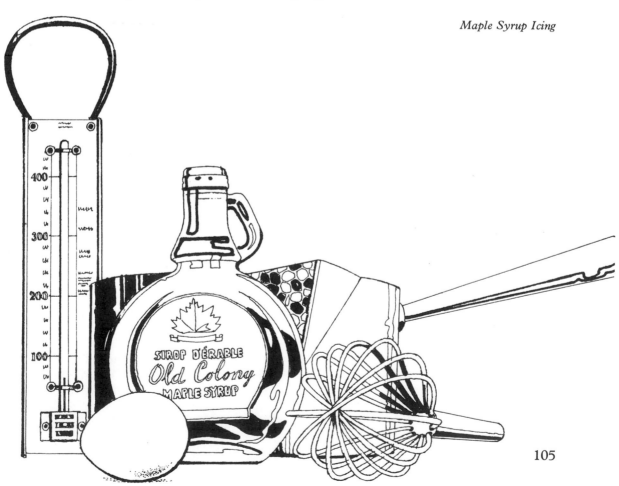

105

Simple Fudge Icing

50 g (2 oz) margarine
50 g (2 oz) cocoa
225 g (10 oz) icing sugar
100 ml (3 fl oz) warm milk

Melt the margarine in a strong pan and add the cocoa. Keeping on the heat add the sugar. Beat in enough of the warm milk to form a good, almost pouring consistency. Use at once for it sets fast. Good on Devil's Food Cake (page 96).

Whisky Filling (1)

50 g (2 oz) butter
150 g (6 oz) icing sugar
30 ml (2 tablespoons) lemon juice
10 ml (2 teaspoons) whisky

Combine the butter and the sugar and beat in the lemon juice and the whisky. Fills one cake.

Whisky Filling (2)

50 g (2 oz) butter
25 g (1 oz) cocoa
5 ml (1 teaspoon) coffee essence
100 g (4 oz) icing sugar
25 g (1 oz) chopped nuts
30 ml (2 tablespoons) whisky

Mix all the ingredients to a soft spreading consistency.

American Frosting

125 g (5 oz) granulated sugar
30 ml (2 tablespoons) water
2 egg whites
1 ml ($\frac{1}{4}$ teaspoon) cream of tartar

Put all the ingredients into a bowl over a pan of hot water. Beat for 7 to 10 minutes over the heat and then remove from the pan. Continue to beat off the heat until the icing holds peaks and is beginning to stiffen. This will top and cover the sides of an 8-inch cake.

Heavenly Filling

50 g (2 oz) butter
80 g (3$\frac{1}{2}$ oz) icing sugar
5 ml (1 teaspoon) instant coffee
10 ml (2 teaspoons) warm water
50 g (2 oz) drinking chocolate
10 ml (2 teaspoons) whisky
25 g (1 oz) chopped nuts

Cream butter and sugar. Mix the coffee powder with the water and add it with the chocolate powder to the creamed mix. Add the whisky and beat all together. Finally add the chopped nuts and use to fill a plain sponge (Bristol or Squeaky).